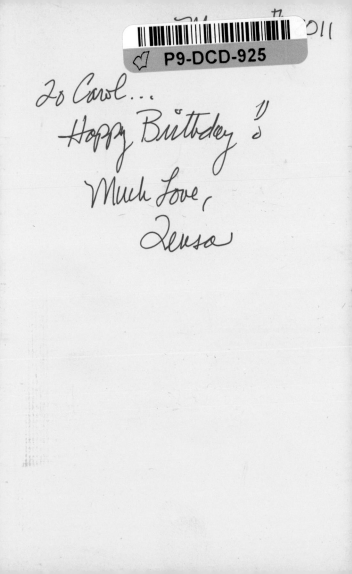

To Carol...
Happy Birthday :)

Much Love,
Lensa

DEVOTIONS *from* GENESIS *to* REVELATION

HEAVEN
CALLING

Hearing *Your Father's Voice*
Every Day of the Year

ZONDERVAN®　　A WORTHY BOOK

ZONDERVAN.com/
AUTHORTRACKER
follow your favorite authors

ZONDERVAN

Heaven Calling
Copyright © 2010 by Worthy Media, Inc.

This title is also available as a Zondervan ebook. Visit www.zondervan.com/ebooks.

This title is also available in a Zondervan audio edition. Visit www.zondervan.fm.

Requests for information should be addressed to:

Zondervan, Grand Rapids, Michigan 49530

Library of Congress Cataloging-in-Publication Data
Heaven calling : hearing your Father's voice every day of the year : devotions from Genesis to
  Revelation.
    p. cm.
    ISBN 978-0-310-33036-3 (hardcover, padded) 1. Bible—Devotional literature. 2. Devotional
    calendars.
    BS491.5.H43 2010
    242'.2—dc22   2010022510

Packaged by Worthy Media. For subsidiary and foreign language rights contact info@worthymedia.com

Produced with the assistance of The Livingstone Corporation (www.LivingstoneCorp.com). Project staff
includes Linda Taylor, Linda Washington, Dave Veerman, Larry Taylor. Typeset by Michelle Muhammad.

Cover and interior design: Christopher Tobias, Tobias Design
Cover photography: © mys/photocase
Interior photography: © istockphoto.com, photocase.com

Printed in China

10 11 12 13 14 15 /CTC/ 20 19 18 17 16 15 14 13 12 11 10 9 8 7 6 5 4 3 2 1

WELCOME

You are cherished. You are chosen. You are called by the hope of heaven to an intimate, life-giving relationship. Are you hearing his voice? Are you living in his love throughout each day? You can, you know.

As you go to work, as you exercise and worship and visit with friends and raise a family, heaven is calling you. Whispering affirmations that comfort you, insights that guide you, and promises that will encourage you each moment on your life's journey.

This inspiring collection of devotions helps you connect personally and uniquely with that heavenly voice as it speaks to your heart from the pages of Scripture. Starting with the richest moments and truths in the biblical story line, we gleaned key verses beginning in Genesis and continuing through Revelation. Each seed verse is followed by a brief devotional that speaks straight to your heart, a suggested Scripture reading, and a short prayer starter—one for each day of the year.

As you take a few minutes each day to tune your ear to heaven's voice, we pray that you will come to know how deeply and personally you are loved. Even more, we pray you *hear* from the One who knows you by name—the One who transforms your heart day by day.

—The Editors

CONTRIBUTORS

Linda Washington

Nikki Studebaker Barcus

Suzanne Burden

Rick Ezell

Carol Chaffee Fielding

Sharla Fritz

Michael J. Klassen

Kathy Lay

Linda D. McGee

Betsy Todt Schmitt

Debbie Simler-Goff

Sandra Stein

Linda Taylor

Jonathan Ziman

JANUARY

JANUARY 1

Then God said, "Let us make man in our image, in our likeness."
—**Genesis 1:26** (NIV)

YOU ARE MY MASTERPIECE

Out of all of my creation, do you know what I consider my masterpiece, my crowning jewel? You. You have great worth in my eyes, beloved. I made the world for you to live in, enjoy, and care for. Each tiny flower, each fluttering butterfly, each vivid sunset is my love poem to you. You are far more valuable to me than the earth, the sky, the animals, and the rest of my creation combined. While you are unique from all other persons, you share similarities: a bit of heaven in your inmost being and my reflection in your life. It was my pleasure to take extra care as I fashioned you from the dust of the earth.

On the days when you feel put down by others, remember that you are precious in my sight. My masterpiece.

Read
Genesis 1:1 – 2:3.

Lord, help me to realize my value to you each day.

JANUARY 2

Then the LORD God called to the man, "Where are you?"
—**Genesis 3:9** (NLT)

IF YOU HIDE, I WILL SEEK

D ear one, long ago I fashioned a people on which to lavish my love. I took on flesh to walk with them each day. My daily times with Adam and Eve were my greatest delight. Yet my anguish was great when they broke the rule I set before them and tried to hide from me, the lover of their souls. In love, I called out to them, to bring them out of hiding. I made provision for them and for their children's children so that no one would ever have to hide from me again.

Child, I know the temptations you face each day, the struggle to follow my rules. When you fail at doing what is right, you want to run and hide. But I will always seek you. I will never let you go, never let you rest in the lie that I no longer love you.

Read
Genesis 2:4—
3:23.

*Jesus, lover of my soul,
thank you for your
willingness to seek me
when I try to hide.*

Then the Lord said to Cain, "Why are you angry? Why is your face downcast?" —
Genesis 4:6 (NIV)

WHY ARE YOU ANGRY?

I love all of my children, beloved. I don't disparage one in favor of another. It grieves me when you believe that I do.

I favored Abel's offering, but did not favor Abel over Cain. Cain misunderstood the difference and allowed his anger to blind him.

My child, I caution all of my children to be slow to anger because of the devastation that anger can unleash. I did not want Cain to go down that path of destruction. Instead of giving in to his emotions, I wanted him to examine why he was angry. Envy was the match that ignited his fury. He chose to hang on to anger instead of me.

Child, when you're upset, don't focus on it to the exclusion of all else. Bring it to me. Let's explore together why you're angry. Then, let's douse that flame together.

Read
Genesis 4:1–16.

Lord, show me the root of my anger. I need your help to deal with it.

JANUARY 4

Make yourself an ark of gopher wood. Make rooms in the ark, and cover it inside and out with pitch. —**Genesis 6:14** (ESV)

IN A BIG WAY

From the beginning, my thought has always been to save my people. First, I made a way to save Adam and Eve when they broke my commandment. Then, in Noah's day, even as I contemplated sending a flood, I came up with a plan to preserve him and his family, along with every kind of animal in the world. An ark—a vessel no one had ever seen before—was my method of choice.

Beloved child, my way of salvation will always be contrary to human expectation. Yet no price is too great for me to pay. I gave my life to save an entire world— something no one would have expected. I also give you the instructions in my Word and the quiet whispers of my Spirit to save you from yourself.

When I save, I save in a big way. That's what a Savior does.

Read
Genesis 6:9–22.

Lord, I am humbled by your way of salvation.

JANUARY 5

Pairs of clean and unclean animals, of birds and of all creatures . . . came to Noah and entered the ark. —
Genesis 7:8–9 (NIV)

GIVE ME YOUR WORRIES

I am strong enough to toss a mountain like a pebble. I am bigger than the universe. So you can absolutely rest your cares safely upon my shoulders.

I know the worries that collect in your life like beads on a string. Sometimes you even add worries that aren't yours to bear. These anxieties sap your energy, beloved. When I gave Noah the task of building the ark, I didn't want him to worry about how the animals would get on board. His job was just to build the ark. My task was to get them there.

Rest assured that I have everything under control in your life too. Just give me your worries, child. In exchange, I'll give you my peace.

Read
Genesis 7.

Lord, I will not worry today. I know you are in charge.

JANUARY 6

When the dove returned to him in the evening, there in its beak was a freshly plucked olive leaf! Then Noah knew that the water had receded. —**Genesis 8:11** (NIV)

IN THE WAITING TIMES

Child, I know how difficult waiting can be. I waited for you to admit your need of a Savior. I wait for you each day to meet with me. So, I know the pain you feel when you wait a long time for something you dearly want.

After the great flood, Noah and his family wondered when the waters would ever recede. The times the raven returned without a sign of greenery added to the weight of their wait. But in my time, the waters dissipated—and Noah's wait was over.

Let's make an agreement here and now, dear one. In the waiting times, offer me your trust. In return, I'll offer you grace, peace, hope—and a guarantee that I'll come through for you.

Is that a deal?

Read
Genesis 8.

Lord, I accept your deal. Grant me the patience to trust your timing.

JANUARY 7

I have placed my rainbow in the clouds. It is the sign of my covenant with you and with all the earth. —**Genesis 9:13** (NLT)

LOOK FOR MY SIGNS

Look around you, child. There are signs of my love for you everywhere. A field of blushing poppies expresses my joy in creating a beautiful environment for you. A rainstorm to water the crops indicates my blessing. A kind word from a stranger . . . that's a sign of my encouragement. A rainbow arcing across the sky . . . that's a display of my faithfulness.

Look for my signs, beloved. You'll find them most evident on your darkest days, when fear or hopelessness are darkening your vision. Some of these signs are attached to things you don't typically welcome. But without the rain, there would be no rainbow. Without the toil of tilling the earth, there would be no flowers or crops.

If you can't find my signs, ask me. I'll point the way with one more sign: my nail-printed hand. It's the expression of my eternal love for you.

Read
Genesis 9:1–17.

Lord, I will look for your signs.

They said, "Come, let us build
ourselves a city and a tower
with its top in the sky. Let us
make a name for ourselves."
—**Genesis 11:4** (HCSB)

YOU CAN REACH HEAVEN

You were made to do great things, child. You are my masterpiece, after all. But you were made to do great things in tandem with *me*—with the Spirit who enables you to do everything in my name.

I never feel threatened by human achievement. In fact, I gave you the intelligence to be the caretaker I called you to be. But human achievement fueled by pride or a desire to subvert my authority saddens me. I watched the people of old build a monument to their own pride, knowing they could never achieve their goal—to reach heaven.

In my grace, child, I sometimes wreck your plans to keep you dependent on me. You can reach heaven, but not by your own efforts. Trust mine instead.

Read Genesis 11:1–9.

Gracious Lord, forgive me for the times when I wander off in pride.

JANUARY 9

*The LORD had said to Abram,
"Leave your country, your people
and your father's household
and go to the land I will show
you."*—**Genesis 12:1** (NIV)

TRUST IS BEAUTIFUL TO ME

What is beautiful to me? I see beauty in a trusting
nature—in a heart that sees me instead of a dark
and unfamiliar path.

Abram trusted me, even though I told him to leave
everything that was familiar to travel to an unknown
place. But I had a reason, dear one. I wanted to bless
my son. I wanted Abram to see the vast, open skies of
possibilities he couldn't even dream of in Haran. I wanted
to give him not just a family but a nation. I wanted him to
have a land so great and plentiful that generations would
weep for joy.

But all of that was yet to come. The first step was
trusting me on the unfamiliar path.

Beloved, your trust in me is beautiful. I have plans
for your good—plans you haven't imagined. Let me behold
the beauty of your faith.

Read
Genesis 12:1–9;
17:1–8.

*Father, I will trust your
voice and follow your
lead today.*

JANUARY 10

Three men were standing opposite
[Abraham]; and when he saw
them, he ran from the tent door to
meet them, and bowed himself to
the earth. —**Genesis 18:2** (NASB)

UNEXPECTED WAYS

I love to visit my children—even when they aren't expecting me. The day two angels and I surprised Abraham and Sarah with a visit was a great delight to me. As was Abraham's custom, he graciously opened his home to me and my companions. He did not ask for anything, but I had a gift for him anyway—the renewed promise of a son.

Think about the people with whom you love to visit. You cherish each conversation, each shared smile. Sometimes, you don't even have to talk—you just want the pleasure of their company. Child, I want the pleasure of your company too. I would love to visit you each day. Each time you open your heart or open the Word, I will meet you there. Just remember that I sometimes come in unexpected ways.

Read
Genesis 18:1–15.

Lord, I long for a visit
from you.

JANUARY 11

*The outcry to the L*ORD *against [the city of Sodom's] people is so great that he has sent us to destroy it.* —**Genesis 19:13** (NIV)

WHEN A FATHER GRIEVES

I grieve every time someone sins. Every time, child. Although my justice and wrath are set in motion when habitual sin takes place, still I grieve.

It also saddens me when my children think that I delight in destruction. My holiness demands justice, yes. But my tears were mingled with the fire raining down on Sodom and Gomorrah. The whole land was polluted by the vice of these communities. A cleansing fire was needed.

Beloved, I am a consuming fire. I cleanse and I refine. Sin cannot stand in my presence. But even as sin meets the fire of my wrath, I grieve as any father would when his child rebels.

Remember my grief, child, whenever you're tempted to stray from me. But remember my fire also. Both are there to lead you back to me.

Read
Genesis 19:1–26.

Lord, forgive me for the times I've caused you grief. Cleanse me, Lord.

JANUARY 12

The angel of God called to Hagar from heaven, "Hagar, what's wrong? Do not be afraid! God has heard the boy crying as he lies there." —**Genesis 21:17** (NLT)

THE GOD WHO SEES

Beloved, I notice everything and hear the cry of every broken heart before it is uttered. When Hagar and Ishmael wandered in the desert, each feeling broken and alone, I was there with them. After all, I sent them there. Even though they were not to be part of the plans I had for Abraham, I still had plans for them. I could never abandon them.

Hagar knew me as "the God who sees." I am the God who sees you, child. Just as I heard Hagar and her son, know that I hear you in your desert place—the place where you have lost hope. I know that lost dream, that agony of despair. Don't give up, beloved. I still have good plans for you and will provide for you.

I will never abandon you.

Read
Genesis 21:8–21.

Lord, I feel alone. I need a sense of your presence to help me hold on.

JANUARY 13

Abraham looked up and saw a ram caught by its horns in the thicket. So Abraham ... offered it as a burnt offering in place of his son. —**Genesis 22:13** (HCSB)

THE REWARD OF TRUST

I watched as Abraham prepared to offer his son—the promised son I had sent. I delighted to see his trust in me, and I rewarded that faith with the very thing he needed—a ram. But I sent that ram not just for Abraham, but for you too. The ram was a promise that one day I would offer up my Son for the provision of all.

I was proud of Abraham that day, just as I am proud of you when you offer me your trust—with nothing held back. I am proud even when you come before me just as you are, with a "Lord, help my unbelief" prayer on your lips. Your honesty is a sacrifice too, child—a sacrifice of pride.

I reward every desire to trust—even when whispered with a shadow of doubt. Because I know that each baby step of trust keeps you following me.

Read
Genesis 22:1–18.

Help me, Lord, to fully trust you.

JANUARY 14

Praise be to the Lord, the God of my master Abraham, who has not abandoned his kindness and faithfulness to my master.
—**Genesis 24:27** (NIV)

I DELIGHT TO SHOW KINDNESS

I am *Jehovah-Jireh*, the God who provides. I provide because I love to show kindness to my people. When Abraham's servant, Eliezer, sought a wife for Isaac, I led him to just the right person. I took seriously my promise to Abraham to craft a nation out of his family.

Child, I know you sometimes doubt my willingness to be kind to you. Those times are usually laced with suffering—when you're tempted to believe that I am changeable and forgetful. As with Abraham, I always desire to be good and gracious to you.

Sometimes I might lead you in paths of suffering to temper your compassion—to inspire you to be tender toward others who find themselves on similar paths. Always remember, though, that I delight to show kindness. Sometimes the greatest kindness I can show you is to invite you to walk the road of suffering with me.

Read
Genesis 24:1–27.

Lord, I want to see you today. Help me to keep my eyes on you.

JANUARY 15

Jacob gave Esau bread and lentil stew; and he ate and drank, and rose and went on his way. Thus Esau despised his birthright.
—**Genesis 25:34** (NASB)

CONSIDER THE CONSEQUENCES

I know your impulses, beloved. They can lead you to acts of compassion or acts of destruction. Esau's impulses led him to forfeit his double-portion inheritance. He sacrificed his future for a moment of pleasure: filling his stomach. His impulsiveness became his downfall.

My child, resist the urge to make hasty decisions, giving up the better things for the lesser things: sacrificing family for career, reputation for status, character for comfort. Instead, weigh the outcome. Rehearse the consequences. Play out the long-term scenario of your actions.

Every decision you make has lifelong implications. So step back. Take a breath and count the cost. And remember: there's always time to talk to me. I can help you make the right decision.

Read
Genesis 25:19 – 34.

I will think before I act today, dear Lord. I will weigh the outcome of my decisions.

What if my father touches me? He'll see that I'm trying to trick him, and then he'll curse me instead of blessing me. —
Genesis 27:12 (NLT)

LISTEN TO MY LEADING

You know that feeling you get when you're going in the wrong direction? You know, the one that almost audibly whispers, *That way is wrong and will have consequences.* That's my Spirit guiding you into truth. I want to steer you away from the negative results of sin and steer you toward holiness and blessing.

Jacob chose to ignore my leading. He participated in his mother's deceptive plan, and his actions caused years of pain for their entire family.

As with Jacob, I know what's best for you, and I want you to experience the best I have for you. So before you take that next step, seek me. And then be ready to listen to my leading. I will bless and guide you with my tender care.

Read
Genesis 27:1–19.

Steer me into righteousness, Father, with your Holy Spirit as a loving guide.

JANUARY 17

I am the LORD, the God of your father Abraham and the God of Isaac. I will give you and your descendants the land.
—**Genesis 28:13** (NIV)

MORE THAN AN INHERITANCE

I long for a close relationship with you. But note that I have children, not grandchildren. Each son or daughter of mine has to know me personally. A relationship with me cannot be handed down through a family.

Rarely do I find a more faithful family than that of Jacob. I called his grandfather Abraham "friend" and entered into a covenant with him. And I blessed Jacob's father, Isaac. Even so, Jacob had to know me for himself. I painted a dream for him. We wrestled. He encountered me in a personal way so I could unleash my work in his life. The same is true for you.

Your spiritual inheritance is important, but secondary. I want to be known as *your* God, not just the God of your ancestors. I value intimacy with you.

Look for me, beloved. I'm waiting for you.

Read
Genesis 28:10–22.

Draw me close to you, Lord. Help me see your worth.

JANUARY 18

Jacob worked seven years to pay for Rachel. But his love for her was so strong that it seemed to him but a few days. —
Genesis 29:20 (NLT)

HOPE IN THE WAIT

I know how hard it is for you to wait. The disappointment seems double when your expectations are not met. You can identify with Jacob in that regard. He worked seven years for Rachel's hand and received Leah's hand instead. The seven years of waiting for Rachel turned into fourteen.

Perseverance ensured that Rachel would become Jacob's wife. But I honored Leah during the wait too. She bore Jacob many children. Six of the twelve tribes of Israel came from Leah's sons.

So when you are frustrated at having to wait, remember that I have my reasons. Trust me. Anticipate what I might have to offer. Meditate on even better possibilities than you hope for and dream.

Jacob could not have imagined that I would build a nation out of the family for which he waited and longed. Joyfully wait for me. You won't be disappointed.

Read
Genesis 29:14 – 30.

Change my impatience to anticipation, Lord, as I trust that something good is brewing.

And Esau ran to meet him, and embraced him, and fell on his neck, and kissed him: and they wept. —**Genesis 33:4** (KJV)

I RESTORE RELATIONSHIPS

Broken relationships are a sad consequence of a fallen world. But rest assured that I am the Master Restorer of relationships. I specialize in mending what has been broken.

The relationship between Jacob and Esau needed to be restored. Years had passed since Jacob had tricked their father into granting him the blessing Esau would have received. But now Jacob was about to encounter the brother whose blessing he had stolen.

You can imagine the fear gnawing at Jacob. But Jacob came to me about it. In humility he asked me to rescue him from Esau. I did that, and more! Their tearful and joyous reunion was far beyond Jacob's expectations.

I wait for you to invite me into situations that need mending too. Are you willing to talk with me about them and wait to see what I can do?

Read Genesis 32:3–28; 33:1–4.

Restore my relationship with _____ to make it glorify you. Grant me the humility to admit my mistakes, Father.

*Let's kill him and throw him
into a pit and say that some wild
animal ate him. Then we'll see
what happens to those dreams.*
—**Genesis 37:20** (CEV)

JEALOUS FOR YOU

My Word describes me as a jealous God. But I'm
not jealous *of* you—I'm jealous *for* you. And a huge
difference spans the two.

Joseph's brothers were jealous of him. He was their
father's favorite son, born of the favored wife. Jealousy
spurred them to impulsive behavior and trouble later on,
as jealousy so often does. I want better for you.

Jealousy *for* someone has love as its driving force.
You love that person so much that you want nothing to
come between you. If something does get in the way,
jealousy properly stirs your soul and flames your passions,
but it's always tempered by patience, compassion, and
complete devotion. Jealousy means being zealous for
another person's good.

That's how I'm jealous for you. I love you that much!

Read
Genesis 37:3–28.

*Lord, take away my
jealousy of others and
make me jealous for
them instead.*

JANUARY 21

Joseph's master took him and put him into the jail, the place where the king's prisoners were confined; and he was there in the jail. —**Genesis 39:20** (NASB)

KEEP TRUSTING

When you struggle to make the right decision and are punished for it, I am still there with you, still there for you. I can take that evil and make good out of it. Just trust me.

Joseph faced a very tempting situation but had the discipline to flee. Doing what was right landed him in prison. Still, he not only clung to me; he also influenced others during his captivity.

Likewise, trust me in your circumstances. My sky-high perspective trumps your ground-zero view every time. I can see far beyond your obstacles and problems. So hang on to me as you wait for your reward. It is coming. Believe. Hope. Remain faithful. And watch for me with anticipation.

Read
Genesis 39.

Lord, increase my faith in the truth that you reward those who obey you.

JANUARY 22

Joseph ... saw that they were
dejected. So he asked [them], "Why
are your faces so sad today?"
—**Genesis 40:6–7** (NIV)

HOPE IN CAPTIVITY

The damp, hard cold of Joseph's imprisonment resonates with you in the midst of your own captivity. Chains of despair or fear or disease squeeze the last vestiges of hope out of your soul. I know what you are going through. You are not alone.

I was with Joseph in prison. He honored me there. When two new prisoners arrived, Joseph didn't keep his distance or threaten them. Instead, he noticed their pain and offered them hope.

I am also with you in your prison. Honor me here. When I send other captives your way, introduce them to me. Share my name with them. Do the work I have for you concerning them. Don't worry about the outcome; that's up to me.

Honor me in your captivity. Even in captivity, you can offer hope.

Read
Genesis 40.

When I'm tempted to
wallow in bondage,
Lord, help me to honor
you instead.

JANUARY 23

The king sent for Joseph, who was quickly brought out of jail. He shaved, changed his clothes, and went to the king. —
Genesis 41:14 (CEV)

SPENDING TIME WHILE YOU WAIT

I know that at times you are tempted to believe I have forgotten about you. But you are my beloved; I could never forget you. You are inscribed on the palms of my hands.

The cupbearer who had promised to mention Joseph to Pharaoh took two years to keep his word. In those two years, Joseph could have easily believed that I had abandoned him. But he didn't. Instead he spent his time with me, honing his faithfulness. And on that anticipated day when Joseph was taken from his murky cell and pushed out into the sun's glare, he acknowledged me before Pharaoh.

Your bondage may end just as suddenly. In the meantime, spend time with me in the shadows. When the brilliant light of deliverance hits your darkened, weary eyes, you will be ready.

Read
Genesis 41:1–27.

Walk with me through my darkness, Father, so that I'm prepared to come into your light.

Pharaoh said to Joseph, "Since God has made all this known to you, there is no one as intelligent and wise as you."
—**Genesis 41:39** (HCSB)

READY FOR SERVICE

Beloved, hardship can be a training ground. It can ready you for service like nothing else will.

Joseph stayed faithful to me in the "boot camp" of prison. He knew and honored my voice. Meanwhile, I groomed him to become Pharaoh's right-hand man and govern Egypt.

Please know, dear one, that I see potential in you that is only fully developed through trials and suffering. I use these difficulties to shape your character and ensure your dependence on me. My intent is to burn away the dross that pollutes the silver that is your life. But always, my intentions for you are good.

I have loved you from the beginning and chosen you for special purposes. But we must walk together—especially through difficulties—so that you can see how relying on me will bring you through anything.

Are you ready to serve?

Read
Genesis 41:37–57.

Train me up in the way I should go so that my service honors your name.

As surely as Pharaoh lives, you will not leave this place unless your youngest brother comes here.
—**Genesis 42:15** (NIV)

JUSTICE AND MERCY

I am a God of justice. I am also the God of love. My will is that justice be lovingly served.

Consider Joseph's situation. Joseph's brothers wronged him by selling him as a slave. Before acknowledging his kinship with them years later, Joseph tested them to see if they had repented of their actions. But Joseph never stopped loving them. Indeed, he forgave them and wept with joy at their reunion. Justice was served in that Joseph ultimately ruled over his brothers—just as I had shown him in his dreams. Yet love restored the family.

You see, precious one, because I love you, I temper justice with mercy. Though my justice demanded the full payment for sin, my mercy caused me to send my only Son to die so that you could have eternal fellowship with me.

Because of my mercy, you don't have to fear my justice. Both are aspects of my love.

Read
Genesis 42:1–21.

I'm so grateful for your loving justice, Lord. May I follow your example.

JANUARY 26

*Send the boy with me. . . . I
personally guarantee his safety.
You may hold me responsible
if I don't bring him back to you.*
—**Genesis 43:8–9** (NLT)

RISKY BUSINESS

I am almighty God. I can do anything. While that can be hard for you to fathom, you show your acceptance of this truth by the risks you take. Taking a risk for me—even in the midst of doubt—shows me that you trust me to work in your situation.

A risk can also mean stepping up and taking responsibility even when doing so is hard. That's what Judah did. He personally guaranteed the safety of his brother Benjamin, even though he had no idea what would happen if Benjamin returned to Egypt with them. Judah was willing to risk his own life to guarantee Benjamin's safe return to their father.

I was with Judah as he took that step of faith. And I will be with you in your steps of faith as well. Take risks, remembering that you walk by faith, not by sight. Risks feel dangerous and make you vulnerable. But that, dear one, is what faith is all about.

Read
Genesis 43.

*God, make me fearless
about taking risks on
your behalf. I trust you.*

It was not you who sent me here,
but God. He made me father
to Pharaoh, lord of his entire
household and ruler of all Egypt.
—**Genesis 45:8** (NIV)

THE GOOD IN THE BAD

I know you've been hurt. You've felt pain, disappointment, and fear amid the cruelty and greed of this fallen world. But I want you to come and seek shelter in my arms. I am working even in the darkness.

Joseph's brothers had sold him into slavery. His feelings of abandonment and betrayal might have festered to the point of rejecting all that is good and right—had he let his feelings take over. But Joseph steadfastly clung to me and my ways through his seasons of despair. Meanwhile, I worked through the despicable actions of his brothers to bring him to the place where he could save their lives.

When evil surrounds you, look for my good. It is there. In gloomy obscurity, seek my clear light. I am there. In only a matter of time you will emerge from sin-steeped circumstance into a beautiful new chapter of your journey. Wait on me.

Read
Genesis 45:1–18.

Lord, when wickedness
surrounds me, help me
glimpse your promise
of hope and a future.

She put him in the basket and placed it in the tall grass along the edge of the Nile River.
—**Exodus 2:3** (CEV)

TAKE COURAGE

When you face obstacles that seem insurmountable, don't be afraid, child. Seek me for courage instead.

Moses' mother feared for her son's life, but she didn't wallow in fear. In faith and with courage she took action—at great risk to herself—believing that I would protect him. I rewarded her trust in me by keeping her son safe.

Moving ahead with boldness releases you from the bondage of fear. Never allow worry or dread to keep you from the wonderful plans I have for you, dear one. With me on your side, nothing needs to send you into a panic. I excel in conquering evil with good!

So take a deep breath. Let my courage infuse you as you take your next step.

Read
Exodus 1:8–16;
2:1–10.

God, remove every trace of fear from me and replace it with your courage.

JANUARY 29

So he looked this way and that, and when he saw there was no one around, he struck down the Egyptian and hid him in the sand. —**Exodus 2:12** (NASB)

I LOVE YOU ANYWAY

Those wrong acts you've done—the ones that you shamefully tuck away in the dark recesses of your memory? I already know about them. I watched as you carried them out.

In spite of your actions, I want you to try and wrap your mind around these crucial facts: I love you anyway. I plan to use you anyway. Even your sin cannot keep me from it.

Moses murdered a man in secret and fled for his life. But my desire to use him in amazing and miraculous ways never waned. He was a chosen vessel to make my power known.

So are you. You have never done anything that would change my mind about that. Just know that I am willing to forgive and cleanse you. Though your sins are like scarlet, they shall be white as snow if only you will come to me with them. Then you and I can face your extraordinary future together.

Read Exodus 2:11–25.

I'm relieved that you've seen it all, and I accept your grace and forgiveness.

JANUARY 30

God called to him out of the bush, "Moses, Moses!" And he said, "Here I am."

—**Exodus 3:4** (NRSV)

MEET ME THERE

I love making myself known to you in vast and varied ways—in a child's sweet hug, a blazing sunset, a stimulating workout, a raging thunderstorm, a song on the radio.

To get Moses' attention, I met him in the form of a bush on fire but not consumed by the flames. Once he was listening, our conversation began in earnest.

I've also tried to get your attention, wooing you in wondrous ways. Follow Moses' example: soak it in. Confirm my reaching out to you by reading my Word and entering into conversation with me. And always, always be on the lookout for me. I will be courting you in a multitude of ways and a multitude of places.

Will you meet me there?

Read
Exodus 3:1–14.

Make me sensitive to your presence, Lord, in both the mundane and the incredible.

JANUARY 31

O Lord, I'm not very good with words. . . . I get tongue tied, and my words get tangled. —
Exodus 4:10 (NLT)

LEAN ON ME

Precious one, do not question my choice of you for the task at hand. If you weren't ready, I would not have asked you to do it.

Instead of giving in to fear of inadequacy, trust me. Rely on me. Lean on me. And just as I did for Moses, I will help you to accomplish what I have called you to do.

I have been equipping you for this task since the day you were born. All of your life experiences have been in preparation for this moment. Act on it, and I will bless your every effort.

Remember, I am a loving Father who wants the best for you. As you step up to the plate, you may feel like a child facing his or her first big game. But know that I will always be the ecstatic Father in the stands, cheering you on.

Read
Exodus 4:1–15.

Lord, infuse me with confidence and empower me to do what you ask.

FEBRUARY

FEBRUARY 1

*Now get to work. You will not be
given any straw, yet you must
produce your full quota of bricks.*
—**Exodus 5:18** (NIV)

THE DEMANDS OF LIFE

My beloved child, I know the difficulties of coping
with demanding taskmasters with ridiculous
quotas. But take heart. There is an end in sight.

Remember, my delays are not defeats. The Egyptians
withheld the straw, but even that had a purpose. So also,
your present struggle has a purpose. You may see your
lack of funds, but I see tangible blessings headed your
way. You may see the unemployment line, but I see the
job I've prepared with you in mind. You may see a difficult
deadline, but I see your creativity and ability to do what is
required.

Precious child of mine, trust that I am always at
work behind the scenes. Your release will come at the
time I have appointed. And when it does, it will be just
as glorious for you as deliverance from Egypt was for the
Israelites.

Read
Exodus 5.

*Lord, teach me to look
expectantly for the time
you've chosen for my
deliverance.*

Then the LORD told Moses, "Now you will see what I will do to Pharaoh."—**Exodus 6:1** (NLT)

A POWERFUL PROTECTOR

Child, envision what I will do on your behalf. I am the Lord your God. Whatever your problem is, I am bigger. I am your Protector. Whoever bullies you will have me to contend with. I am your Refuge. No force in the universe is greater than me. I am the source of all power. I speak and the thunder rolls. I clap my hands and lightning flashes.

The enemy makes a lot of noise, but has no real power. I have already decided how your enemies will be defeated. Now I want you to be a part of their defeat.

Do not cringe when I ask you to face the opposition. I am the same God who was with Moses when he came before Pharaoh. Rest assured that I am with you also and have prepared the words for you to say.

With me by your side, your adversaries will do whatever you command them to do.

Read
Exodus 6:1–12.

Sovereign Lord, your great strength and power gives me great comfort and peace.

*The Egyptians will then know
that I am the LORD when I
stretch out My hand against
Egypt.* —**Exodus 7:5** (HCSB)

RECOGNIZING THE REDEEMER

Child of mine, do you know that even the most difficult people in your life recognize that my favor is upon you? Their pride may prevent them from saying so, but deep down they know you are mine.

Sadly, this irritates them, and causes them to retaliate against you as the Egyptians retaliated against my people Israel. But be encouraged. I see their hard hearts and I will raise you up to a place of prominence before their very eyes. I will see to it that you walk in victory, while they walk in defeat.

Though I bring miraculous signs and wonders to your community, still they will not repent of their wicked ways. Soon, they will be crushed because they refused to yield to me. And although that will grieve me, it will be a needed warning to all who refuse to relinquish their hearts to me.

Read
Exodus 7:1–13.

*Lord, keep my heart
soft. I never want to
experience the suffering
that stubbornness
brings.*

FEBRUARY 4

The magicians said to Pharaoh,
"This is the finger of God." But
Pharaoh's heart was hardened,
and he would not listen to them.
—**Exodus 8:19** (ESV)

A TEACHABLE HEART

I have all power, but I am judicious in my use of it. I could have easily destroyed Egypt on the way to freeing my people. But I chose to give Pharaoh a choice. His choice was to refuse to yield to me. All of my wonders only made his heart grow harder.

I was grieved then, and I grieve now when I see the same hardness in people today. Their pride leaves no room for me—even when I rock their world.

Precious one, when situations happen beyond your control, remember that I am sovereign—fully in control of all circumstances. Don't allow pride, anger, or stubbornness to come between us. If you let me, I can help you keep your heart teachable and humble. I always respond to a humble heart.

Read
Exodus 7:14–20;
8:1–19.

Sovereign Lord, teach
my heart to have the
right response to your
mighty acts.

FEBRUARY 5

Then Pharaoh . . . said, "Go,
sacrifice to your God here in
the land." But Moses said, "That
would not be right." —
Exodus 8:25–26 (NIV)

NO COMPROMISE

My child, I know your struggle with the temptation
to compromise. It goes hand-in-hand with a desire
for convenience and control. But I want you to recognize
the temptation for what it is—and look to me to help you
resist.

Pharaoh's desire to compromise was clear to Moses—
Pharaoh wanted to release my people on his own terms.
But I had instructed Moses that my people should go deep
into the desert to worship me.

Moses understood that such a half-hearted attempt
at obedience—on Israel's part or on Pharaoh's part—is the
same as disobedience. This attitude of compromise never
works with me.

Beloved, I have one exciting surprise after another
planned for you. But just as an earthly father knows that
the sweetest rewards come with obedience, I too have
some requirements—obedience without compromise.

Read
Exodus 8:20–32.

God, help me to joyfully
do all that you ask.

FEBRUARY 6

The heart of Pharaoh was hardened, and he did not let the people go. —**Exodus 9:7** (NASB)

A HEART OF FLESH

Spotting someone's audacious refusal to obey me is easy, isn't it? Pharaoh's livestock was dead, many of his men lay dead in the streets from the hail I sent, and his own body was covered in boils. Yet Pharaoh still raised his fist to me.

Many who read of Pharaoh's response shake their heads—even though they have acted in the same way. Every time someone flippantly disregards a minister's biblical admonition—he disregards me. Every time my Spirit convicts a person and she refuses to change—she dishonors me.

You see, dear one, a heart doesn't always grow hard over big issues. Often the smallest issues develop the deepest roots and lead to longstanding attitudes of bitterness and resentment. The good news is, I can turn a stony heart into a heart of flesh. Remorse brings repentance, and that is always my goal.

Read Exodus 9:1–26.

I humble myself before you now, Lord. Forgive my attitude and past actions.

FEBRUARY 7

*I've also done it so you can tell
your children and grandchildren ... and so you will know
that I am the LORD.*

—Exodus 10:2 (NLT)

TELL THE STORY

Remember when you first realized who I was? What
an exciting day that was for both of us! I will never
forget your joy when I made you my own.

I love for my children to talk to others about me—to
share their stories of the mighty acts I have done for
them. Your story helps others know that I am real.

I wanted Moses and my people to testify of how
I delivered them from Egypt. That is why I allowed
Pharaoh's heart to harden. As I told my servant Moses, I
already knew that Pharaoh would not change. The longer
he delayed the Israelites' departure from Egypt, the more
I could demonstrate my power. And the more I did this,
the greater impact the Israelites' story would have on
future generations.

Go ahead, child. Tell the story—tell *your* story of my
works—and watch what I will do as you step out in faith.

Read
Exodus 10:1–23.

*Jehovah God, teach me
to transmit your truths
in exciting ways to my
children.*

The LORD will pass over your home. He will not permit his death angel to enter your house and strike you down. —
Exodus 12:23 (NLT)

DISTINCTION

My beloved, how favored you are! You are one of my precious, chosen ones—separate and distinct. Because of that, I delight in protecting you and providing for you as I provided for my people Israel

When you fully embrace your calling as my child, you enjoy great benefits: You will have peace in the midst of calamity—just like the Israelites had peace when the death angel passed over Egypt. Some of the world's plagues will not touch you—just as some of the plagues did not affect the Israelites. And I will cause your enemies to bless you—just as I caused the Egyptians to give my people silver and gold.

Celebrate that you are unique and beloved. I rejoice over you.

Read
Exodus 11:1–7;
12:21–36.

Lord, help me to fully grasp what it means to be favored by you.

FEBRUARY 9

Moses said to the people: "Do not be afraid. Stand still, and see the salvation of the LORD, which He will accomplish for you today."
—**Exodus 14:13** (NKJV)

THE WALL OF FEAR

I am the good Shepherd who delights in protecting his sheep. No matter how loudly your enemy blows out threats, no matter how utterly impossible deliverance seems, I will rescue you in the nick of time. I rescued Moses and my people at the Red Sea, though they doubted me. In their fear, they believed that the Egyptians had them trapped. The real culprit, however, was fear.

Don't let fear be a wall that keeps you from me. Know that I will never fail you. Remember that the worse your situation is, the more glory I receive for turning it around.

Your present situation is not about you at all—it's about me, and about my will and my purpose in this earth. Relax, child; I love you. And like a fierce lioness protecting her cubs, I always come out fighting on your behalf.

Read
Exodus 14.

God, when I'm fearful, please wrap your strong arms around me and comfort me.

FEBRUARY 10

He cried out to the Lord, and
the Lord showed him a tree;
and he threw it into the waters,
and the waters became sweet.
—**Exodus 15:25** (NASB)

ASK FOR HELP

My child, when the waters of life seem bitter, talk to me and see what I have for you

Moses cried out when my people complained in the desert. They only saw the size of their need, not my ability to provide. They forgot that I created water to sustain life, and that I always delight to supply what my people need.

Just as I demonstrated my power when the Israelites sojourned in Egypt, I showed them my power in the desert. Let me do the same for you. When you're facing similar situations, be quicker to ask for help than you are to complain. And remember that I am always here when you need me. I can turn things around, my child. I can turn those bitter situations sweet.

Read
Exodus 15:22-27;
17:1-7.

Lord, if I start to
complain, please help
me to remember how
powerful you are.

In the evening you will have meat to eat, and in the morning you will have all the bread you want. —**Exodus 16:12** (NLT)

THE PROBLEM SOLVER

You always have an open invitation to bring any problem to me. I am your heavenly Father and I know what you need. You will face no problem that is too difficult for me to solve.

When my people demanded food in the desert, I gave them bread so that one day they would recognize my Son as the bread of heaven. Likewise, I give you food—your daily bread—and keep you safe and help you when things go wrong. My pleasure is to give you what you need today and every day.

Even when you think I'm not here, I'm as close as your next breath. This is my promise to you.

Read
Exodus 16.

Lord Jesus, open my eyes to see how great and capable you are.

FEBRUARY 12

Moses' father-in-law said to him,
"What you are doing is not good.
You and the people with you will
certainly wear yourselves out."
—**Exodus 18:17–18** (ESV)

THE GIFT OF OTHERS

I made my people to love each other and to work in
concert. Yet so many times I've seen you striving to
accomplish tasks all by yourself.

I do not expect anyone to be a one-person show, and
I don't want you struggling under the strain of it all. My
intention was never to weary you in your calling, child.
I gave you your gifts and intelligence so that you could
mentor others who can assist you.

Moses' father-in-law gave sound advice: choose
people of integrity and talent to serve under you. Let
them help you bear the burdens of leadership. I can't wait
to see the sparkle in your eyes and the spring in your step
once more as you take my words to heart.

Enjoy the ministry I gave you. Delight in it. And
realize my special gift to you in all of this is the gift of
others.

Read
Exodus 18.

Wise Father, thank you
for giving me the gift of
relationships.

FEBRUARY 13

Now if you obey me fully and keep my covenant, then out of all nations you will be my treasured possession. —**Exodus 19:5** (NIV)

A TREASURED POSSESSION

Though Israel was the smallest among the nations, I chose her as my treasured possession. My people had only to obey me; I would be their God and Protector forever.

You are also my treasure—a priceless diamond. I lovingly gaze at you in the morning while you are still asleep. I quietly speak with you on your way to work. I walk with you through the busyness of the day, and sit with you in the still of the evening. I'm delighted when you spend time with me, and proud when you obey me.

My commands are designed to make you the best you can be. My statutes set you apart from those who do not know me. They protect and guide you.

People will try to convince you that my demands are too great, or that my motives are selfish. But know that, whatever I ask, it's because I love you. You are priceless to me.

Read
Exodus 19.

Abba Father, I want to make you proud of me today and every day.

Honor your father and mother.
Then you will live a long, full life
in the land the LORD your God is
giving you. —
Exodus 20:12 (NLT)

BOUNDARIES

My child, I am a God of order. The boundaries I have established provide order in this fallen, chaotic world. They were not given to hinder your freedom but to show the joy and rewards that come with living within their safety. With great care, therefore, I determined what behaviors would bring my people contentment. And I shared these in the Ten Commandments.

Each commandment was carefully written with my own hand. And as you heed each one, you will discover my bountiful blessings. Some rewards are clearly spelled out for you, like having a long, full life if you honor your parents. Others you will realize fully when you are with me in heaven.

Beloved, consider these boundaries as an act of love. I want to keep you safe and whole. Obedience helps you stay that way.

Read
Exodus 20:1–17.

Loving Father, thank you for the wise boundaries you have set for me.

FEBRUARY 15

*"Come on," they said, "make
us some gods who can lead us."*
—**Exodus 32:1** (NLT)

WHO ARE YOU FOLLOWING?

My love for my people is boundless—far deeper
and wider than you can ever imagine. I rescued
Israel—my treasured possession—from slavery in Egypt. I
guided my people step by step, night and day. When they
were thirsty, I provided water. When they were hungry,
I gave them bread made in heaven. And I grieved when
they turned from me to worship something worthless,
something made with their own hands.

Likewise, I grieve when you put anyone or anything
before me: a promotion, financial security, a relationship.
Beloved, cast aside all earthly "gods." Let me lead you
on a better path. Like I did for my children in the desert,
I will guide you and provide for your every need. Follow
me, and I will show you a path lined with peace, love,
mercy, and grace.

Read
Exodus 32:1–20.

*Lord, help me turn
toward you. Show
me the way, so that
I may follow you
wholeheartedly.*

Moses did everything just as the LORD commanded him.
—**Exodus 40:16** (NIV)

LET US WORK TOGETHER

Do you think that I needed someone to build me a home on earth? Look up at the night sky. The expansive heavens are my tent. The stars shine exactly where I placed them. The world and all its wonders exist because I spoke and made them so. When I gave Moses my instructions for building the tabernacle, it wasn't because I couldn't do it. No, I gave Moses the task because I wanted him to join me, to help build my people into a great nation.

Loved one, I have a task that only you can carry out. I offer you an opportunity to make a difference in this world that will have everlasting significance. All that is needed is your willingness and your obedience to do the work. I do everything else.

Won't you join me?

Read
Exodus 40.

Open my eyes, God, to the work that you have for me. Give me the ability to obey.

FEBRUARY 17

[Miriam and Aaron] said, "Has the LORD spoken only through Moses? Hasn't he spoken through us, too?" —**Numbers 12:2** (NLT)

NO PLACE FOR ENVY

I love all of my children equally—no favorites. Yet they sometimes fail to understand this. This was as true in ancient Israel as it is today. Next to Moses, Aaron and Miriam represented the most powerful people among the Israelites—the priests and the prophets. Moses relied on them. Yet they envied his power and position as leader of the people. I disciplined them for their sinful and destructive attitude, as any loving parent would.

Dear child, envy has no place in my family. I have given each of my children wonderful gifts, talents, and abilities. You are uniquely and wonderfully made. So when you become envious of what someone else has, are you not tearing down and disrespecting what I have put into place?

Envy does not build up or encourage; it only destroys. Don't allow it to have a foothold in your heart. Understand and rest in my love for you.

Read
Numbers 12.

Dear God, protect my heart and mind from envy and jealousy.

FEBRUARY 18

The other men who had explored the land with him disagreed. "We can't go up against them! They are stronger than we are!"
—**Numbers 13:31** (NLT)

WHAT DO YOU SEE?

Child, my faithfulness isn't some airy promise, but a truth as solid as a mountain. When I vowed to give my people Israel the land of Canaan as their inheritance, I meant to keep that promise. Yet they couldn't see beyond the fortified cities and the powerful people inhabiting those cities. Only two of my chosen ones—Caleb and Joshua—had the right perspective. They believed that with me leading the way, they could do anything.

I long for you to believe that too, my child. When you are confronted by a seemingly overwhelming obstacle—a lost job, a spouse who has left, an illness that can't be treated—pause and consider: what do you see? Do you see a hopeless situation, or an opportunity to allow me to work in and through your life?

I am there in the pain. I am there in the troubles and the difficulties. And I will be with you in the Promised Land.

I promise.

Read
Numbers 13:1—
14:4.

Lord, when I am overwhelmed by my situation, help me to see you in my trouble.

The whole assembly talked about stoning them. —
Numbers 14:10 (NIV)

THE CROWD MENTALITY

When I look at my children, I don't see a crowd. I see each person and the qualities that make him or her unique. That's why it grieves me when my sons and daughters look at their peers with a longing to be like them or to think like them.

I know the fears that drive my people to give in to the crowd. It was easier for the people of Israel to go along with the spies who trusted their eyes than to stand in faith, trusting my promises. Yet Joshua and Caleb did just that. They chose to stand alone and affirm my presence and power to a multitude who could see only fear and failure.

Today, I want you to remember that you are not alone. Instead of looking at the problem, look to me. I am with you.

Read
Numbers 14:5–45.

Forgive me when I go along with the crowd rather than stand for you and my faith.

FEBRUARY 20

Make a replica of a poisonous snake and attach it to a pole. All who are bitten will live if they simply look at it!

—**Numbers 21:8** (NLT)

LOOK TO ME AND LIVE

I am the Source of life. I'm overflowing with it, like a fresh-running stream. Those who look to me and follow me will find abundant life.

My people the Israelites needed to learn this lesson. They grumbled as they wandered through the desert, despising the very food I provided for their nourishment. So I sent poisonous snakes as punishment for their unbelief. Even then, I offered them a way to repent and be healed. And it was simple: look at a snake made of bronze, and you will live. This was a reminder for them to look to me and live.

I offer you the same opportunity. Look at my beloved Son. Keep your eyes fixed on him. He offers you true life. Obey and live.

Read
Numbers 21:4–9.

Heavenly Father, help me be obedient today and keep my eyes focused on your Son.

FEBRUARY 21

The Lord opened Balaam's eyes, and he saw the Angel of the Lord standing in the path with a drawn sword in His hand.
—**Numbers 22:31** (HCSB)

OPEN YOUR EYES

Beloved, my greatest delight is to see my children grow in faith. I reveal myself through my Word and my deeds, but some revelations are a product of my displeasure. Balaam had been blinded by the promise of riches. So I sent my angel to stand in his way and open his eyes.

I cherish the steps my children take toward me. But when they advance on a path that leads to destruction, I sovereignly place roadblocks in their way as an act of mercy, not manipulation.

Child, I want you to grow, but not grow distant. Remember that I can see all avenues—as well as your blind spots. When you're confused, stop and ask me to open your eyes. I will show you the right path.

Read Numbers 22:4–34.

Father, let me not be blinded by my desires to pursue the wrong way.

FEBRUARY 22

*The hidden things belong to the
LORD our God, but the revealed
things belong to us and our children forever.* —**Deuteronomy**
29:29 (HCSB)

THE HIDDEN THINGS

Loved one, I have given you a vast capacity for
curiosity and wonder. I love your desire to learn,
explore, and grow in knowledge. Yet there are some
"hidden things" that I have chosen not to reveal to you
on this side of heaven, just as I chose not to reveal every
detail of my plans for my people Israel.

Some things are simply unnecessary for you to know.
Moses understood this truth—and trusted me anyway.
So trust me in this: everything that you do need to know
in order to live faithfully is written plainly in my Word.
Everything you need to know about me—about what I
require of you, and how much I love you—is right at your
fingertips.

And that's no secret.

Read
Deuteronomy
29:2–29.

*Thank you, Lord, that
you have given me all
I need in order to obey
you and know you.*

FEBRUARY 23

I have set before you life and
death, blessing and cursing;
therefore choose life, that both you
and your descendants may live.
—**Deuteronomy 30:19** (NKJV)

THE CHOICE IS YOURS

From the beginning of time, beloved, I chose you. I have loved you and have held your best interests close at heart, but I will not force you to choose me. The decision to obey me or reject me is yours, just as it was for my people Israel. But don't be misled, child. This is not a decision about where you will live, or what career you will pursue, or what your next major purchase will be. This choice is a matter of life and death. Choose me, and you will choose life—an abundant life, filled with my love, my grace, my mercy.

I am life! I offer it to you freely. Choose me—and live.

Read
Deuteronomy 30.

This day I affirm that
I choose you, God. I
choose to love and obey
you this day.

Do not be afraid.... For the
LORD your God will personally
go ahead of you. He will neither
fail you nor abandon you.
—**Deuteronomy 31:6** (NLT)

COURAGE FOR THE ROAD AHEAD

Do *not be afraid.* This is not a command given lightly, as if you will surely fail at the task. Rather, it is a command to focus on what is true. I gave Moses and my people this command to encourage them to trade fear for faith. They could choose to not panic because I would be with them as they entered Canaan.

When I call you to a new job or relationship, or place you in a situation where your next step is uncertain, be strong and courageous and wait for my lead. I am with you, my child. I will not fail you, neither will I leave you on your own.

Together, we can conquer whatever lies ahead.

Read
Deuteronomy
31:1–8.

Lord, help me choose
faith instead of fear.

*The LORD knew Moses face
to face and sent him to do
signs and miracles in Egypt.*
—**Deuteronomy 34:10–11**
(NCV)

MISSION IMPOSSIBLE?

I know you, child—your strengths and weaknesses. I also know your beliefs about what you can or cannot do. As a father has compassion for his children, I have compassion for you. Yet I wouldn't be a good Father if I didn't know when to stretch your limits.

Initially Moses balked when I called him to go to Egypt—he wanted to hide behind his limited abilities. My abilities have no limits. Through my power Moses could perform miracles.

Precious one, trust me to know what you can and cannot do. Whatever task I call you to, I will give you exactly what you need to do it—just like I did Moses. Together, we will accomplish great things, just as Moses and I did.

All you need to do is listen and obey. Just like Moses.

Read
Deuteronomy 34.

*Father God, help me to
be faithful today to the
task you have called
me to perform.*

Be careful to obey all the instructions Moses gave you.... Then you will be successful in everything you do.

—**Joshua 1:7** (NLT)

TAKE ME AT MY WORD

My words are never spoken in haste, and never without purpose. I always speak with a full knowledge of what's true. My word always accomplishes my purposes.

Although Joshua faced the daunting task of leading little Israel to conquer the Canaanites, I bolstered his courage with truth. I had promised my servant Moses that I would give my people the vast territory beyond the Jordan, and I repeated that promise to Joshua. No one would be able to stand against the Israelites if Joshua would only take courage and faithfully follow my instructions.

Loved one, I know exactly what you are facing today. I am with you, just as I was with Joshua and my people. If I tell you to be strong and courageous, take me at my word; I will enable you to be successful in whatever your circumstances.

Read
Joshua 1.

God, sometimes I don't feel strong or courageous. Help me today to trust in you.

FEBRUARY 27

*Please swear to me by the
LORD that you will show kindness to my family, because I
have shown kindness to you.*
—Joshua 2:12 (NIV)

A HEART OF FAITH

I choose to look at the heart of a person rather than
the outer shell. Take Rahab. While people saw a
prostitute—a woman used and scorned by others—I saw a
woman of faith and honored her for that. Wherever faith
like that exists, I can work with and through that person
to accomplish my goals—whether one is a shepherd boy,
a teenage girl, a tax collector, or a persecutor of my
disciples.

A humble heart filled with faith always draws me,
beloved. Your belief that I can do wonders in your life is
precious to me. Even with faith the size of a mustard seed,
you can see me accomplish the impossible. Loved one,
simply believe and acknowledge that I am God.

That's all you need.

Read
Joshua 2.

*Lord, give me the faith
today to know that you
can use me to fulfill
your purposes.*

FEBRUARY 28

As soon as . . . their feet touched the water's edge, the water from upstream stopped flowing.
—Joshua 3:15–16 (NIV)

TAKING THE FIRST STEP

My child, I am the Creator. I set the clouds in motion and the sun and moon in place. I snap the winds like whips and tame raging seas. Folding back the waters of the Red Sea or stilling the floodwaters of the Jordan River has always been child's play to me.

All I required of my people Israel at the Jordan was for them to step into the river. This act of faith was the first necessary step toward taking the land. When they moved, I moved.

Beloved, I am still in the business of doing amazing works among you. You just have to take the first step in faith and obedience. The best way to do this is to keep your eyes on me, not the floodwaters of your circumstances. When you move, I move. Are you ready?

Read
Joshua 3.

Father God, in this difficult situation I am facing today, help me to take that first step.

MARCH

MARCH 1

*When you hear them sound a
long blast on the trumpets, have
all the people give a loud shout;
then the wall of the city will
collapse.* —Joshua 6:5 (NIV)

WINNING STRATEGY

Child, I love it when you walk with me. I know
that sometimes the path I put before you seems
strange—it certainly did to my people as they prepared
to battle Jericho. I called Joshua and the Israelites to a
literal walk of faith: I would give Jericho into their hands
if they followed my instructions. I had my reasons—and
they obeyed, neglecting not one command. In faith, they
conquered that city.

If what I am asking you to do right now doesn't make
much sense, let's talk. I don't mind your questions. I know
you sometimes struggle to understand my ways. In the
end, what matters to me in any situation is that you are
faithful and that, despite your questions and doubts, you
trust me.

Go ahead; step out with me. When we walk together,
we succeed.

Read
Joshua 5:13 – 6:20.

*Lord, my life right now
doesn't make sense.
Give me the faith to be
obedient.*

MARCH 2

I will not remain with you any longer unless you destroy the things among you that were set apart for destruction. —
Joshua 7:12 (NLT)

MY PROTECTION

My protection is like a sheltering umbrella. When you stay under that umbrella, you remain safe and dry. Sometimes the umbrella takes the form of me asking you to obey certain commands—even when those commands seem petty or unimportant to you. Achan thought that just a little sin would go unnoticed. He did not really know me very well.

But you do. You know that it took my Son's death to deal with sin—so no sin is little or goes unnoticed. But because of that sacrifice, you and I can have a relationship.

I wanted that so much. I didn't want sin to separate us. And because of Jesus' death, it won't; he covered all sin. But until the end of time, when I completely eradicate evil, my umbrella is here to help you stay away from the things that would hurt you.

Let me protect you. Let me draw you close. Let me keep you safe and dry.

Read
Joshua 7:1–13.

God, help me remain in your constant care by obeying you quickly and completely today.

MARCH 3

Do not be afraid of them; I have given them into your hand. Not one of them will be able to with-stand you. —**Joshua 10:8** (NIV)

AN ALMIGHTY CHAMPION

My child, I'm well aware of the battle you're facing. I see you lying awake at night, worrying, fretting, working out combat scenarios in your mind. You're in a difficult situation—but I specialize in those. I love to show my power when the odds are stacked against you. Turn your anxious thoughts into prayers and invite me into your battle. I long to be your champion.

I will go before you and fight for you. I'm on your side, guiding, strengthening, empowering. Just as I went with Joshua, and even answered his prayer to make the sun stand still, so I will help you.

Remember, I am almighty God—your champion. The victory is already yours. Ask me for what you need, and ask it boldly. Let me show you what I can do.

Read
Joshua 10:1–15.

Almighty God, I pray that you go before me, with me, and behind me into every battle I face today.

So take diligent heed to yourselves
to love the LORD *your God.*
—**Joshua 23:11** (NASB)

PRIORITY ONE

*L*ove me. That's what I want. Joshua understood this.
That's why, when he gave his farewell speech, he
reminded my people to be diligent about loving me.

That seems like an odd juxtaposition of words,
doesn't it? But I know human nature, and how loving me
can sometimes fall to the wayside. How even my own sons
and daughters can take my blessings for granted.

I don't want you to do that, my child. Take heed
to love me. Remember to love me. When I am your top
priority, everything else in your life will fall into place.
When you love me, your mind will be focused on what
really matters.

You are always at the forefront of my mind. Let me
be at the forefront of yours.

Read
Joshua 23.

Lord, I love you.
Always. Forever. Help
me to be diligent in
loving you.

MARCH 5

The people said to Joshua, "We will serve the Lord our God. We will obey him alone."

—**Joshua 24:24** (NLT)

WORTHY OF DEVOTION

Beloved, you aren't stuck in your old life of darkness, fear, and hopelessness anymore. I have freed you from bondage and rescued you from death. You have witnessed my miracles in your life.

I have given you a new life filled with light, abundance, and promise. You have experienced victory through the power of my Spirit and been blessed with goodness you didn't have to slave to acquire. I have transplanted you from the land of want into a land teeming with plenty—everything you need.

I've provided you with both a history and a legacy. What do I ask in return? To honor me with your obedience, just as my people Israel promised to do.

Serve me with your life. You are my greatest treasure.

Am I yours?

Read Joshua 24:2–31.

You are worthy of my obedience and devotion, O God. I will serve you with my whole being today.

MARCH 6

Up! For this is the day in which the LORD has delivered Sisera into your hand. Has not the LORD gone out before you?
—**Judges 4:14** (NKJV)

ASSURANCE OF VICTORY

I have promised to never leave nor forsake you, my child. That includes when I call you into battle. I am a trustworthy leader. I don't give my recruits an assignment and then stand by and watch them fail. I painstakingly prepare my soldiers for every fight. Victory is assured when you put your confidence in me as your commander-in-chief.

My servant Deborah told Barak that I was going ahead of him to give my people success. She did not focus on the enemy's numbers or their might; she knew they were no obstacle for me. Her faith gave Barak courage.

So quiet your fearful heart, dear one. I have not lost sight of you. In fact, I have gone before you. I know all the strategies of the enemy and will teach you how to defeat every scheme.

I won't leave you to fight on your own. You and I together—we're invincible.

Read
Judges 4:4–16.

I take my focus off the battle and put it on you, Lord God.

MARCH 7

*Please, Lord, how can I save
Israel? Behold, my clan is the
weakest in Manasseh, and I am
the least in my father's house.*
—Judges 6:15 (ESV)

FIT FOR BATTLE

C hild, when you call me, I will answer you. When you
feel like everyone—anyone—is better suited to the
task, I will prepare you. When you tremble in your boots,
I will strengthen you. When the world laughs at you and
mocks you, I've got your back. You call yourself weak; I
call you my mighty warrior.

Gideon doubted my call because he didn't fit the
popular criteria for a warrior—powerful, courageous, self-
assured. But I often call the weak and timid because I can
show my greatness through them.

When you are doubtful and need assurance, I will
be patient. Though your heart melts with fear, go in the
strength that you possess, and I will fill in the gaps. I
want to show you, and those watching, what I can do with
a willing heart.

Read
Judges 6.

*Lord, I am weak, but I
am willing to be used.
Make your power
evident through me.*

MARCH 8

If you are afraid to attack, go down to the camp . . . and listen to what they are saying. Afterward, you will be encouraged.
—Judges 7:10–11 (NIV)

ENCOURAGED

Child, I am the God of encouragement. I know that you become fearful when you can't see what lies ahead. But fear is not from me. Give it to me, and once your hands are free, place them in mine. I will lead you on the path marked out specifically for you.

Gideon was afraid. I understand why. The odds against him seemed insurmountable. I knew that he needed encouragement—a certain kind of encouragement. And though I like it best when my children don't doubt me, I can work with them where they are in their faith. I gave Gideon what he needed, and it helped him to no longer be afraid.

Keep following my way and I will lead you on amazing adventures. And if, like Gideon, you need encouragement to keep going, I will supply that too.

Read
Judges 7:1–14.

Holy One, today I wait with eyes open to see how you address my concerns and fears.

Then [Gideon] returned to the
Israelite camp and shouted,
*"Get up! For the L*ORD *has given*
you victory over the Midianite
hordes!" —**Judges 7:15** (NLT)

BE READY TO BE AMAZED

When the battle is at hand, child, rest assured that I will be with you to the finish. Because I am such a creative God, I may bring about your victory in a very unusual way. Nonetheless, I will give you the victory.

Gideon had only a few men, some trumpets, and jars with torches inside. But that was enough to rout the enemy. Certainly not a common way to go into battle, but I am not a common God and I do not work in common ways.

Watch for my surprises. The battle plan I have may be beyond your imagination, with a solution or strategy that you never considered. I love to do that—to solve problems in ways no one ever thought of.

When the battle is at hand, child, rest assured that I will be with you to the finish. Enter in, and be ready to be amazed.

Read
Judges 7:15 – 25.

Lord, the odds seem
overwhelming, but I
will trust you. Lead on!

MARCH 10

Now drink no wine or similar drink, nor eat anything unclean, for the child shall be a Nazirite. —**Judges 13:7** (NKJV)

PERFECT PURPOSES

I created you to have a life of purpose. To ensure this, I have given you rules and boundaries. People sometimes get upset about what they see as my stringent demands. They don't understand that my rules are born out of love—just as a loving father sets limits to protect and guide his child.

For some leaders in the Bible, I gave special instructions to highlight their call to holiness. With Samson's mother, I required a vow to show that her son was my choice to deliver the nation of Israel—led by the power of my Spirit.

I have called you for a special purpose as well. You may not be aware of what I'm calling you to do, but rest assured that I am preparing you—in fact, I have been all along. Let me be your loving Father. Love and trust me enough to hear and obey.

Read
Judges 13.

Father God, I will find rest and security in the boundaries you give me, remembering that they serve a purpose.

*His father and mother objected.
. . . "Why must you go to the
pagan Philistines to find a wife?"*
—**Judges 14:3** (NLT)

VOICES OF WISDOM

I have given you resources to guide you: my Spirit, my Word, and a discerning heart. I have also placed older believers in your life to help you. These spiritual mentors see you for who you really are—weaknesses too—and love you anyway. They care about you because they have invested in you. They want the same thing for you that I do—life in abundance.

Samson's parents tried to warn their son. They understood that I did not want my chosen people intermarrying with the unbelievers around them because of the many problems it would cause. Sadly, Samson refused to listen to the wisdom of his parents—and the results were disastrous.

The older, godly people in your life have experienced much, and what they can teach you is priceless. Listen to their advice. Seek their counsel.

After all, they love you almost as much as I do.

Read
Judges 14:1–11.

*Lord, show me to
whom I should listen
for advice.*

*Then the Spirit of the LORD
came upon [Samson] in power.*
—**Judges 14:19** (NIV)

MULTIPLIED

My child, I want you to be involved in my purposes right here in your world. I have given you my Spirit to equip you. I have supplied you with spiritual gifts as well. Some gifts are meant to be used out in front; others behind the scenes. Some gifts touch many people; others only one or two. Your spiritual gifts are my hands and feet right where you live.

Although Samson was my child, he didn't always act as I desired. But he did accomplish many tasks for me, and my Spirit helped him.

My Spirit is your Helper too. I will show you the gifts I have given you, and will guide you in developing those gifts so that you can fulfill my purposes. And you have this assurance as well: when you invest your time, treasure, and talents in service to others, I promise to multiply your efforts.

Read
Judges 14:12–20.

*Reveal in me the gifts
you've given, and show
me how to use them for
your purposes today.*

MARCH 13

Because she nagged him day after day and pled with him until she wore him out, he told her the whole truth. —
Judges 16:16–17 (HCSB)

YOUR CONSTANT GUIDE

S amson had every opportunity . . . His parents tried to tell him not to get involved with Philistine women, but he wouldn't listen. And later, when he met Delilah, his love blinded him to her schemes. She showed her hand several times, but Samson just couldn't see what she was up to.

When you stay close to me, my child, I can guide you through your sometimes-confusing world. I can help you avoid the potholes on the road of your life and open your eyes when a situation isn't quite right.

My purpose is to give you life to the fullest and to protect you from harm's way. When you stray, you make yourself vulnerable to others' deceptive schemes. But when you stay close to me, I give you my guidance and protection, as well as life overflowing.

That's how much I love you.

Read
Judges 16:4–20.

Thank you for every good thing you've given Me. Lord, I present each gift back to you as an offering.

Sovereign LORD, remember me
again. O God, please strengthen
me just one more time.
—**Judges 16:28** (NLT)

AS SOON AS YOU CALL

It broke my heart to see Samson that way—blinded, in chains, brought out to a party to be mocked by the Philistines. He often went his own way, but still, I had plans for him to accomplish. So when he prayed that one last prayer, I heard and answered in a mighty way.

My child, if you have strayed from me, know that I have not strayed from you. I'm here. Like the father of the prodigal son, I am eyeing the horizon, watching for your return. My ears strain, listening for the faintest sound of your voice. As soon as you call my name, I'll hear you and come running to your side.

It doesn't matter what you've done. It doesn't matter where you've been. My Son died to handle all of that. What matters is that you return to me.

Read
Judges 16:21–31.

Help me not to wait,
Lord. May my first
response be to turn to
you.

MARCH 15

I went out full, and the LORD has
brought me home again empty.
—**Ruth 1:21** (NKJV)

POINT OF LIGHT

My beloved child, I am well acquainted with grief,
and I readily recognize it in you. You have lost
much, and your heart is in tatters. But realize this: you
have not lost me.

I have counted every tear coursing down your
face. I have been there through every sleepless night. I
have not abandoned you—I am the same God who has
loved you and provided for all your needs. Your present
circumstances do not change my character. Your pain does
not erase my goodness or cancel out my faithfulness.

I felt Naomi's grief and emptiness, so I gave her a
point of light in her dark sky—her daughter-in-law, Ruth.
Look around, my precious one. Find that bit of light in
your dark sky—that little blessing from me. I have not
forgotten you. I have given you what you need to keep going.

Look for me.

Read
Ruth 1.

Even in my distress,
you provide everything
I need. Thank you,
Lord. I will trust in
you.

*I also know about everything
you have done for your mother-
in-law since the death of her
husband.* —**Ruth 2:11** (NLT)

THE ONE WHO SEES

I love this story. I love how Boaz listened with interest
to the back-story of Ruth, this newcomer to the
village of Bethlehem. I watched him watch her and drew
the two of them together at just the right time.

You may sometimes feel like no one notices you, but
I do. I saw you during those days you toiled and received
not so much as a thank you. I was there during those
nights when you sacrificed sleep for another's benefit. I
know the times you did without in order to put someone
else's needs first. I am aware of every time you gave a
gentle answer and swallowed your pride.

You have been a faithful friend. Most of all, you have
done your best to imitate me. I've noticed; you've made
me very proud.

Well done, my faithful servant.

Read
Ruth 2.

*Lord, if the only voice
of gratitude that I hear
today is yours, that will
be enough.*

"I will do whatever you say,"
Ruth answered.

—**Ruth 3:5** (NIV)

TRUSTED COUNSELORS

Child, I know you desire guidance, and I want to give it. I haven't left you to struggle and wonder; I don't delight in your confusion. But if I were to lay out the entire plan of your life in front of you, you couldn't handle it—it would be too much. So in my grace, I only show a little of the path at a time. I give you enough light for the next step.

My Holy Spirit will guide you, as will the wise counselors I place in your path. How will you know them? My appointed advisers don't merely listen to my Word, they do what it says. And they know me. My servant Ruth trusted Naomi's word for these very reasons. And I honored that trust with great blessings.

I will do the same for you.

Read
Ruth 3.

Thank you for the
trusted counselors in
my life. May I always
heed their advice.

MARCH 18

*The women said to Naomi: "Blessed is the L*ORD* who has not left you without a redeemer today."* —**Ruth 4:14** (NASB)

UNEXPECTED

I delight in taking what the world sees as useless and making it strong and vital.

Naomi went to Moab "full"—her entire family intact—and returned to her homeland empty. But I didn't leave her that way.

She thought she had nothing left. She felt I had abandoned her. But I wasn't finished.

I looked upon her in love and filled her to overflowing, restoring what she had lost—a family. I provided a way and a future for her, taking that which was broken and making it new again. She couldn't see what I had in mind for her, but she was always on my mind.

On those days when you feel too weak to be useful to me, read my promises. I take joy in filling the empty, strengthening the weak, finding the lost, embracing those who feel abandoned.

I delight in doing the unexpected.

Read
Ruth 4.

Lord, do the unexpected in my life today.

MARCH 19

If you will look upon my sorrow and answer my prayer and give me a son, then I will give him back to you. —
1 Samuel 1:11 (NLT)

WILL YOU KEEP YOUR PROMISE?

My precious child, what a joy it is when my children keep their word! I saw Hannah's anguish over the pain of her barrenness. All of heaven witnessed her cries for a son and the promise she made. All of heaven rejoiced when she was faithful to keep her promise.

She did not have to promise anything, but I'm delighted that she did. When she brought her son to the tabernacle in fulfillment of her vow, it was hard for her to let him go. Yet she trustingly released him to my care, and in turn, Samuel was able to fulfill the great plans I had for him.

Keeping a promise is not always easy. My promise to save the world by sending my Son was not an easy one either. But I kept my word. I love it when my children keep theirs. It shows that they are learning to be like me.

Read
1 Samuel 1.

Lord, I will keep my promises and be faithful to you.

*Samuel said, "Speak, for your
servant is listening."*
1 Samuel 3:10 (NIV)

HAVE YOU HEARD?

With Adam I spoke face-to-face. With Elijah, I spoke in a whisper. Paul heard me speak from a blinding light. Samuel didn't recognize my voice at first; but once he knew it was me, he was ready for my message.

Have you heard my voice lately? In the loudness of life you may not hear me calling. But I do beckon you—in your conscience and in the depths of your heart; when you read my Word and when you pray.

I love it when we talk. I love it when you quiet yourself—even amid the noise—and spend time with me.

One day, we'll talk face-to-face! But until then, keep listening for my voice. If you pay attention to mine, you won't confuse it with other voices in this world, for I speak only what is true, just, lovely, and pure.

Precious one, tune your ear. I am calling to you. Come talk to me.

Read
1 Samuel 3.

*Lord, I will listen to
your voice and read
your message in your
holy Word.*

MARCH 21

The people refused to listen to Samuel. "No!" they said. "We want a king over us."

—1 Samuel 8:19 (NIV)

I KNOW WHAT IS BEST

You may not always understand, child, but I have your best interests at heart. Think back to all those times when you prayed and prayed for something. At times I answered with a yes. Occasionally I said no. And a few prayers remain yet unanswered.

I know what lies ahead for you. I have guided you toward certain decisions and warned you against others, for your benefit. I did the same for my people Israel—warning them about the consequences of selecting a king. Still, they demanded one on their terms. And my people were never the same.

Though you are prone to push ahead and ignore my warnings, I will continue to respond "yes," "no," or "not yet" out of love for you. When you trust me with the answers, I will rejoice with you in your successes. And when you fail to heed me, I will grieve with you, and then urge you to keep moving forward, never forgetting the lessons you've learned.

Read
1 Samuel 8.

Thank you, Lord, for guiding me each day. Help me to pray for your will in my life.

MARCH 22

*I've just thought of something!
There is a man of God who lives
here in this town. . . . Let's go
find him.* —**1 Samuel 9:6** (NLT)

JUST IN TIME

Dear one, your life contains no coincidences. You are mine, and I have ordered your days in such a way that each one consists of a series of divine appointments. Apt words are spoken when you need them. Provision is made just in time. You "suddenly realize" what the next step should be at just the right moment—all courtesy of my sovereignty and my Spirit.

Perfect timing and perfect provision are exactly how I helped Saul and his servant cross paths with Samuel. It was all in my plan. Now if you'll only trust that I have everything under control in your situation too . . .

Beloved, the next time you are surprised at how things "just happen" to work out, remember that it was no coincidence—everything in my care occurs for a reason. Then let your surprise become praise as you watch me work all things together for your good, just in time.

Read
1 Samuel 9:1–17.

*Open my eyes, Lord.
May I see how you have
made everything work
together for my good
and your glory.*

Samuel took a jar of olive oil and poured it on Saul's head. He kissed Saul and said, "The LORD has appointed you to lead his people." —1 Samuel 10:1 (NCV)

EQUIPPED AND READY

I take pleasure in choosing people to do my work and then empowering them to fulfill it. I create each person with a unique personality that moves them toward a certain type of work. When they heed the desire I place within them, they learn the skills necessary to do the job well. And as they choose to follow me, I bestow gifts that demonstrate their true proficiency for what I have called them to do.

I gave my people the king they desired—Saul—and provided him with all he needed to lead my people well. But above all, I gave Saul my Spirit so that he could fulfill my calling. Likewise, it is my delight to equip you for the work to which I have called you.

Rest easy. With my Spirit guiding you, you are the best one for the job.

Read
1 Samuel 10:1–24.

Thank you for giving me a purpose, Lord. Help me to do the work you have for me to the best of my ability.

MARCH 24

Nothing can hinder the Lord from saving, whether by many or by few. —**1 Samuel 14:6** (NIV)

I AM ON YOUR SIDE

Beloved, I know you sometimes feel as if no one is on your side, especially when you are the only person standing for what is right. But you are not alone. In fact, as my child, you are *never* alone. Jonathan knew my power and strength and relied upon me when he was vastly outnumbered by the Philistines. With my help, he overcame the enemy.

Come to me with your battles and your fears. The size of the problem does not affect my ability to act. With me at your side, you will conquer the problems that once seemed insurmountable! Remember, for me nothing is impossible.

Read
1 Samuel 14:1–23.

Lord, when I feel alone in my battles, help me to remember that you are by my side.

*The LORD doesn't see things
the way you see them. People
judge by outward appearance,
but the LORD looks at the heart.*
—1 Samuel 16:7 (NLT)

THE HEART OF THE MATTER

I can see the tiniest microorganism and the farthest
star millions of light-years away. I am everywhere
at once. So I do not judge as humans judge—based on
subjective criteria: appearance, wealth, status. None
of these impress me. I look at the heart instead, the
intentions of a person. And my wisdom is perfect, child; I
am not arbitrary or subjective.

While Samuel was surprised at my choice for king, I
chose David because I knew his character and values—his
was a heart in tune with mine.

As with David, I have chosen you to do my work.
There's no need to fear—*I know you.* I formed you in your
mother's womb and have loved you from the very moment
your life began. Your innermost thoughts are not hidden
from me; I know what makes you tick and what makes
you sing.

My heart cherishes you, dear one. I long for you to
know and cherish me. Just bring me your heart.

Read
1 Samuel 16:1–13.

*I want to know you
better, Lord. Help me to
take the time to learn
more about you.*

MARCH 26

You are not able to go out against this Philistine and fight him; you are only a boy, and he has been a fighting man from his youth.

—1 Samuel 17:33 (NIV)

A MATTER OF PERSPECTIVE

I see everything with perfect clarity, my child—and I offer clarity to you. I am never clouded by doubt, worry, or prejudice. I know the end from the beginning. You can rely on my perspective.

Saul failed to rely on me—and his vision was clouded by fear. In contrast, David saw the enemy from my point of view and knew he could be victorious with my help.

Are you looking at problems through your perspective, or mine? On your own, you see an insurmountable mountain—a "giant" of a problem—while I see a tiny dot on the roadmap of your life. From my vantage point, the problem pales in comparison to the solution I've provided.

I'm here to help you see your way clearly—all the way to victory. Rely on me to see you through.

Read
1 Samuel 17:1–37.

Help me to see through your eyes, Lord, that my vision may be clear.

David defeated the Philistine with a sling and a stone.... He struck down the Philistine and killed him.

—1 Samuel 17:50 (HCSB)

THE TOOLS FOR VICTORY

When I created you, I knew your purpose, and I provided you with skills and gifts unique to you.

David was meant to be a giant-slayer. Some felt he couldn't accomplish that purpose without certain tools—Saul even tried to place his tools in David's hands. But David knew that I had provided him with exactly what he needed to get the job done: five smooth stones, a slingshot, and a whole lot of faith. He was victorious, and I was glorified.

Likewise, I have equipped you to accomplish your purpose. Beloved, I wouldn't send you into the world without what you need to succeed. Not only have I given you the right tools, but I promise to be right beside you every step of the way.

Read
1 Samuel
17:38–52.

Thank you for providing me with everything I need to accomplish your purpose for my life.

David continued to succeed in everything he did, for the LORD was with him.

—1 Samuel 18:14 (NLT)

A HUMBLE HEART

I love a humble heart. Consider the example of my Son. In humility, he gave up everything to be with you on earth—all to fulfill my will. His earthly forefather, David, had a similar heart, intent on glorifying me in everything he accomplished.

My child, whether I ask you to give your all or whether I give you great success, be humble. You don't need people acknowledging your sacrifice or applauding your success—knowing I am proud of you should be enough!

Dear one, you won't ever go wrong when you center yourself in my will. Because of your dedication to me, I can hold you up for others to emulate. And as long as you are humble, others will follow your example.

In your humility you bring me honor. In your success you bring me glory. Your willingness to be used to further my kingdom brings me great joy.

Read
1 Samuel 18:5–30.

Lord, any success I have is all due to you. Please help me to remain humble.

MARCH 29

Jonathan had David reaffirm his oath out of love for him, because he loved him as he loved himself.
—1 Samuel 20:17 (NIV)

LOYALTY

I know the cost of loyalty, dear one. My loyalty to you cost me my Son, who gave his life for you. In Jonathan's case, he had to make a choice between his friend and his father. In a supreme act of loyalty, he did as I asked and protected his friend David, even at the risk of Saul's wrath.

Such faithfulness is rare between humans, but it is a way of life with me. You can always count me as your most loyal friend. I am the friend who sticks closer than a brother. In fact, I love you so much that I sent my Son to save you from eternal separation from me.

No matter what you are facing, I will always be true and protect you from the evil one. And I'll never betray you. You can count on it.

I LOVE U JESUS

Read
1 Samuel 20:1–17.

Today + + +

I thank you, Lord, for being my loyal friend. Help me to always stay true to you.

*Go in peace, for we have sworn
loyalty to each other in the
L*ORD*'s name.*

—1 Samuel 20:42 (NLT)

ALWAYS

I keep my promises, beloved. I also honor the
covenants my people make in my name. Long after
generations pass, I remember and uphold those covenants
because I am eternal.

The covenant of friendship is especially dear to me.
I honored Jonathan and David's vow of loyalty, even after
Jonathan's death.

A covenant of friendship is never wasted, child. Even
if a friend proves less than loyal, I know your heart, and I
remain steadfast and true. You never have to worry about
my commitment to you.

Dearest one, I have promised never to leave you
or forsake you, even in the worst of times. That is my
covenant to you. Always.

Read
1 Samuel
20:18–42.

*Lord, thank you for
your steadfast and
enduring friendship.*

This day you have seen with your own eyes how the Lord delivered you into my hands.
—1 Samuel 24:10 (NIV)

MY WHISPER

I know the constant clamor of voices that vie for your attention—friends who think you should do one thing, coworkers who think you should do another. These voices sometimes drown out my whisper. People may want to help, but good intentions don't always equal good advice.

When you need guidance, wait for me to advise you, child. Go to a quiet place, away from the chatter, and talk to me first. I'm your ally, and I'm here, waiting for you to come to me! The size of your dilemma is no problem; I will help you make a decision through the counsel of my Spirit—and sometimes through the counsel of advisers I send your way.

Don't let the impulses of your peers sway your life-choices. Instead of looking to those around you, look up. Seek me first. And wait for my whisper. I will show you the way.

Read
1 Samuel 24.

I'm grateful, Lord, that I can come to you for direction in any decision—large or small.

APRIL

APRIL 1

Praise be to the LORD, the God of Israel, who has sent you today to meet me. May you be blessed for your good judgment.
—1 Samuel 25:32–33 (NIV)

WISE CHOICES

Dear one, I created you with an amazing mind. Your brain controls so much involuntarily—your heartbeat and your breathing, for example. Yet an array of actions and thoughts are completely voluntary: you choose what you say and do. How much better it is to choose wisely and to do right.

David asked for something reasonable; Nabal responded with rudeness; David sought vengeance. This would not have ended well for anyone. Nabal's wife, Abigail, recognized the foolishness of her husband's decision and set about making things right. Her quick thinking kept David from actions he would have later regretted and, incidentally, saved the lives of her husband and his servants.

When my children think first, act wisely, and seek peace, I am pleased. I long to give you wisdom in every situation, my child. Just ask.

Read
1 Samuel 25:1–35.

Thank you, Lord, for giving me the wisdom to do what is right.

APRIL 2

He asked the LORD what he should do, but the LORD refused to answer him, either by dreams or by sacred lots or by the prophets.
—1 Samuel 28:6 (NLT)

LIGHT AND LIFE

Saul didn't make just one decision that put distance between us. Sadly, it happened over a long period of time. I reached out to him repeatedly, but he refused my advances.

I am calling out to you, my child. *I love you!* But when you don't listen to me, when you sin and don't repent, when you close off parts of your life to me, you build walls between us. I stand aside and wait—I won't just barge in. But my desire is for us to stay so close that the moment a wall starts to rise between us, you will sense me reaching out to you and we can take it down together.

Child, listen, follow . . . and open even the darkest parts of yourself to me. I'm here to bring you light and life.

Read
1 Samuel 28:3–19.

Lord, I want you to bring light into my darkness and have my heart forever.

APRIL 3

*David realized that the Lord had
confirmed him as king over Israel
and had blessed his kingdom
for the sake of his people Israel.*
—2 Samuel 5:12 (NLT)

WITH YOU

When you were a child playing your favorite game with your favorite friend, I set you there. When you developed your first crush, experienced the flutter of infatuation, and fell in love with someone who loved you too, I set you there. When you stood with the wind in your hair and the sun on your face at ocean's edge, I set you there. At each moment of your life, I have been right there with you.

My servant David had no idea he would become king of Israel as he tended sheep all those years. But I placed him on the throne to shepherd my people.

My dear child, you can't imagine what I am preparing, but I also have surprises for you. In this moment in time, remember: I have placed you where you are for a special purpose. And I am with you always. Even to the end of the age.

Read
2 Samuel 5:1–12.

*Thank you that when
you set me in place, you
stand right with me.*

"Don't be afraid!" David said. "I intend to show kindness to you because of my promise to your father, Jonathan."
2 Samuel 9:7 (NLT)

SENSITIVE CARE

I was proud of my servant David. He could have perceived Mephibosheth—the last surviving member of the previous dynasty—as a threat, or even done as other kings would and had him killed. But David had made a promise to Mephibosheth's father, and David sought to fulfill it. That's what my true servants do.

Many friends have passed through your life. Some of them offered great encouragement and helped you in your walk with me. Like David, perhaps you could take a moment today to check in on those friends—or even their loved ones. I will guide you as to who needs to hear from you right now.

Let's talk.

Read
2 Samuel 9.

Show me who needs my encouragement today.

APRIL 5

The thing that David had done
displeased the LORD. —
2 Samuel 11:27 (ESV)

WITH ALL YOUR HEART

My beloved, we both know when you've done wrong. The walls you build between us during those times sadden me. What hurts most, though, is when you blame someone else for your actions or pretend that I cannot see what you have done.

I want to give you my joy, peace, and love so that you can experience all the blessings of a restored relationship with me. When you are dealing with sin, my child, trust me, I've seen it all. All my children have sinned, and I loved them right through it. David committed murder and adultery, and still I did not give up on him. He didn't want to talk to me at first, but I broke through anyway—and the wall between us gave way to an even deeper intimacy.

Nothing is too big for me to forgive—my Son's blood took care of everything. I made sure of that. So come. Seek me. I long to forgive and bring you back to myself.

Read
2 Samuel 11.

Thank you for being a God of mercy and grace. I need both.

APRIL 6

David said to Nathan, "I've sinned against the L<small>ORD</small>." And Nathan said to David, "The L<small>ORD</small> has also taken away your sin." —2 Samuel 12:13 (NASB)

IT'S COVERED

When you sin, it really doesn't make sense for you to try to hide from me. I see you. I know you through and through. I know what happened. So come and talk to me. When you admit your part, it opens the door to my forgiveness.

I sent Nathan to coax David out of hiding—for I simply loved David too much to overlook his sin. David confessed, and I forgave. He did face some consequences, but he and I were able to work through them together.

I love you too much to leave you in your sin. When you confess it to me, it is covered; I don't see it anymore. Bring your sin to me, and we'll nail it to the cross, where it can stay forever.

Read
2 Samuel 12:1–25.

Thank you for your gracious forgiveness.

*Suddenly Amnon's love turned
to hate, and he hated [Tamar]
even more than he had loved her.*
—**2 Samuel 13:15** (NLT)

I AM STILL HERE

I am deeply saddened by the sin in the world. Though Amnon committed his evil act centuries ago, it reads like today's headlines. That's because sin never really changes. Neither do its consequences. But I'm here to help you even through those consequences.

I haven't abandoned you; instead, I want you to continue to walk with me, trusting that I can work in all situations to redeem things for good. I can take what Satan thought would destroy you and turn it upside down, enabling you to help others who face similar difficulties.

Beloved, I am here. Always. Even when bad things happen—difficult, horrible things—continue to put your trust in me.

Read
2 Samuel 13:1–19.

*Father, help me to
see that you are with
me even in the most
difficult times.*

APRIL 8

Absalom spoke to Amnon neither good nor bad, for Absalom hated Amnon, because he had violated his sister Tamar. —
2 Samuel 13:22 (ESV)

FATHER GOD

I created people to need and love one another. That never changed, even when sin entered into the world. Yet in spite of my desire for loving harmony, families often make a mess of their relationship.

I warned David that his sin would cause problems within his family. Ultimately, after simmering and planning for two years, one of David's sons killed the other in vengeance for their sister. If only they had sought me in the process . . . I love to help families secure and strengthen their bonds.

I believe in family. I believe in family so much that I'm building an eternal home for mine. Meanwhile, I'm right here in the midst of your earthly family—and my heart's desire is to help you come together in peace and mutual love. Just call on me for guidance. After all, I'm a Father. I want to help my children.

Read 2 Samuel 13:20–39.

Heavenly Father, guide me in my family relationships.

David said to all his officials
who were with him in Jerusalem,
"Come! We must flee, or none of
us will escape from Absalom."
—**2 Samuel 15:14** (NIV)

FIGHT OR FLIGHT?

I am the source of wisdom. I gladly share my wisdom to help you choose your battles, beloved.

There are times to confront, times to ignore, and times to flee. My servant Joseph fled to resist Potiphar's wife. My servant David, after sensing the hearts of his people turning against him, chose to flee from his son, Absalom, rather than to do battle with him.

Sometimes the wisest thing to do is flee the situation. But don't ever leave me behind! When others sin against you, don't retaliate—run right into my arms; I am the Prince of Peace. When you are pursued by fear, head straight for me—your refuge and strength; I will protect you.

As you seek the shelter of my wisdom, you will know when it is time to join with me and fight—and when it is time to leave the battle entirely in my hands. Let me show you what is best.

Read
2 Samuel 15:1–23.

Father, show me when
it is best to flee from a
difficult situation.

The man answered, "I wouldn't touch the king's son even if you gave me twenty-five pounds of silver." —2 Samuel 18:12 (NCV)

THE LITTLE THINGS

The man in this account stood against Joab and chose to do what was right. My child, at any given moment you may have a difficult choice to make. That's why every day, in even the smallest situations, I like to show you the right path and see you follow it.

I rejoice when you are my hands—showing my love to those around you, helping the needy and lonely. I delight when you take up my voice—squelching rumor and gossip, telling truth, speaking encouragement. I celebrate when you follow my advice—avoiding situations that tempt you, spurning a love of material things, seeking what is pure and excellent.

You see, when you are faithful in the small things, you will know the right thing to do and you will have the strength to do it when a dilemma presents itself. You also bring me joy.

I really love it when you treat the little things as being important. That is when you shine.

Read
2 Samuel 18:1–17.

Lord, teach me to be faithful even in the small things.

*His father had never interfered
with him by asking, "Why
do you behave as you do?"*
—1 Kings 1:6 (NIV)

IT'S A TOUGH JOB

Because of David's sin, trouble never left his household. He gave his children everything except discipline. The results of permissiveness were written on the life of his son Adonijah.

As a Father, I understand the fine lines of parenting. When discipline is neglected or abused, I see the results: the devastated child who hears too many critical words; the insecure teen who fails to experience unconditional love; the self-absorbed twenty-something who believes the world revolves around his or her comfort and desires.

Yet I know that sometimes, even when parents do everything right, children experience difficulty. All you can do is your best. That's all I ask.

Being a good parent takes energy, time, and attention. My Word is full of wisdom for raising and dealing with children. Let's talk about those children right now. After all, I love them too.

Read
1 Kings 1:5–27.

*I pray for the children
in my life, Lord. Help
me be the parent I need
to be for them.*

APRIL 12

All the guests of Adonijah were terrified; and they arose and each went on his way. And Adonijah was afraid of Solomon.
—1 Kings 1:49–50 (NASB)

MY PATH FOR YOU

Dear one, if you walk with me every day, you'll have wisdom for your journey. And if you'll remember to come to me before making decisions, you will avoid some hazards along the way. This was a lesson that Solomon's brother did not learn, and his scheme to be king led to his death.

So often my children make their own plans apart from me. They run on ahead without consulting me first, and before they know it, they've lost their way. My desire is to show you the fulfilling path I have marked out for you; then you won't waste time racing down other trails that end in frustration.

When you draw near to me, my Word, and the wise counsel of Christian friends, I will set you on the path I prepared for you all along. I would much rather help you avoid disaster than pick up the pieces afterward. I have far better plans for you.

Read
1 Kings 1:28–53.

Lord, I want to follow you and your plans for me.

APRIL 13

I ask that you give me an obedient heart so I can rule the people in the right way and will know the difference between right and wrong. —**1 Kings 3:9** (NCV)

BOLDLY ASK

As a Father, I know how to give good gifts to my children. I painted the night sky with stars and carpeted the fields with sweet-smelling grasses and flowers. But I am especially happy to give generously when my children make bold requests—requests that are rooted in my desires and plans.

Solomon could have asked for patience, world peace, or the end of poverty—all good requests. Or, like many people, he might've chosen something fleeting—like health or wealth. But he chose my rich guidance in leading my people—something that was perfectly in line with all that he knew of my heart. And I blessed him beyond all expectations.

Because I am the source of wisdom, using wisdom makes me a partner in your plans. Let's team up, starting today.

Read
1 Kings 3:2–15.

Lord, today I pray for wisdom to carry out your will in your way.

They held the king in awe,
because they saw that he had
wisdom from God to administer
justice. —**1 Kings 3:28** (NIV)

WORKING SIDE BY SIDE

Solomon used the wisdom I gave him to effectively govern his people. Likewise, I have given you special gifts to respond to the needs you see.

The needy are everywhere, and as my hands and feet, eyes and ears to the people I've placed around you, you are custom-made to do my work. Side by side, you and I will brighten your little corner of the world.

I know that sometimes the task seems so large and your ability to help so small. Just remember that I am here to assist you in even that small part. You won't be able to meet every need—only I am capable of that—but you can do something. That is all I ask.

No matter what I call you to do, know that I will be with you. I love it when you work alongside me in this world.

Read
1 Kings 3:16–28.

Father, I love working
by your side. Thank
you for trusting me
with your work.

APRIL 15

If you obey all my laws and commands, I will do for you what I promised your father David. —**1 Kings 6:12** (NCV)

A MATTER OF THE HEART

Long ago, Solomon followed my very detailed specifications and built a temple for me. It was precisely the right length, height, and width. It had the exact number of rooms I requested and was built out of the specific materials I designated. As a reward, I renewed my promise to the Israelites: to live among them and be their God.

I was pleased with Solomon's obedience, just as I am pleased with your obedience, my child. I rewarded Solomon not just for his compliance but for his heart. His deepest desire was for my will to be accomplished—and he gave himself to it, heart and soul.

When you are confused by the details of what I ask you to do, talk with me. Ask me for clarity. I am intimately involved in the details of your life, as well as the master plan. When your heart's desire matches mine, nothing can stop you.

Read
1 Kings 6.

My heart's desire is that your will be accomplished. Use me, Lord.

When the queen of Sheba heard
about the fame of Solomon . . . she
came to test him with difficult
questions.

—1 Kings 10:1 (NASB)

WISE AND DISCERNING

My child, be on your guard. Many people are teaching nice-sounding messages—but messages that are contrary to my Word. Instead of blindly following along, follow the example of the queen of Sheba and test the wisdom of the teachers you hear. Do a little checking before you accept their lead. Not everyone who says they have found "the way" are even on the right road.

Look into what these teachers believe about my Word—if they trust it to be inspired, holy, and true. Find out what they think about my Son and if they understand who he is and what he did for them. Then see how their lives match up to what they say they believe.

I know it can be confusing out there; a lot of voices are vying for your attention. Just keep your focus on me—the Way, the Truth, the Life—and I'll do the rest. I will help you to be wise and discerning.

Read
1 Kings 10:1–13.

Give me discernment
to follow the teachers
who are truly yours.

APRIL 17

Rehoboam rejected the advice the elders gave him and consulted the young men who had grown up with him and were serving him. —**1 Kings 12:8** (NIV)

WISE COUNSEL

My child, I am glad for you to seek counsel in your decision making. But even then, it takes discernment to know which advisers are best—especially when their advice conflicts. Rehoboam had that problem. He had two sets of counselors: some young men who were his friends, and some elders who had served his father, Solomon.

People who have walked with me for many years can be one of your greatest resources. Are you willing to draw near and hear them out?

It may happen that your peers have wisdom beyond their years, but don't neglect those older saints who know me well. Their advice should point you back to me and the things I've told you in my Word. When it does, hide it in your heart, and then come and talk with me. I will always help you make the final decision.

Read
1 Kings 12:1–19.

Surround me, Lord, with those who know and honor you.

APRIL 18

*How much longer will you waver,
hobbling between two opinions?
If the Lord is God, follow him!*
—1 Kings 18:21 (NLT)

MY OFFER, MY LOVE

My love is true. I loved you even before you knew
me, and I still love you today. As one of my
own, I yearn for you to know me. But like anyone who
truly cares about you, I am unwilling to force you into a
relationship with me; I want you to freely accept my love.

I offer the same choice to you as I did to my people
long ago. Instead of wavering between opinions, Elijah
asked them to choose. My people had been unsure about
the power of the idols that surrounded them in the land.
Was I really the one true God? Many ask that question.
Am I worth their complete devotion?

I don't want you to have to wonder, my child. Will
you choose today to walk wholeheartedly with me?

You will never be sorry.

Read
1 Kings 18:17–29.

*Lord, reveal yourself to
me. I want to know you.*

*Now when all the people saw it,
they fell on their faces; and they
said, "The Lord, He is God! The
Lord, He is God!"* —
1 Kings 18:39 (NKJV)

FILLED TO OVERFLOWING

It took a mighty miracle—but my people finally understood that, indeed, I am God and there is no other. Sometimes that's what it takes to make people see me. Nonetheless, I am willing to do whatever is needed to draw them back to me.

I see the sadness that fills the world today, and I long for this generation to return to me as well. The god named Baal is long gone, but my heart breaks at what people worship as their gods: money, possessions, power. If only they understood that these things eventually lose their value and leave a soul even emptier than before.

I, however, do not disappoint or lose my value. I am the Lord everlasting, and no one cares about you more than I do.

Try me and see, child. See for yourself: my love will satisfy you, filling the emptiness in your heart to overflowing.

Read
1 Kings 18:30–39.

*Lord, fill my heart
with your love.*

After the earthquake came a fire,
but the LORD was not in the fire.
And after the fire came a gentle
whisper. —**1 Kings 19:12** (NIV)

MY COMFORT AND CARE

Sometimes my servants need extra comfort and care—
oddly enough, especially after times of success. After
Elijah's victory on Mount Horeb, he fell into the depths of
fear and depression. Understanding that he needed to hear
from me, I met him right there in the cave, tended to his
needs, and then called to him in a gentle whisper. I still
had work for him to do. But for the moment, I wanted him
to rest.

You're not expected to be "on" at all times either,
my precious servant. I know that success can lead to
exhaustion—which gives rise to doubts and fears. What's
more, Satan hates it when you succeed, and he will try
to discourage you. In those times, I will care for you in
double measure.

Stop for a moment and listen. Hear my gentle
whisper. Doubt and fear won't hold you back, for I still
have work for you to do. But right now, just rest.

I am here.

Read
1 Kings 19:1–13.

Lord Jesus, let me hear
your gentle whisper
when I face doubt and
fear.

APRIL 21

Naboth replied, "The LORD forbid that I should give you the inheritance that was passed down by my ancestors."
—**1 Kings 21:3** (NLT)

STAND STRONG!

In my love for you I have given you the words of life to direct your steps and keep you safe. The laws I give are for your good—they are purposeful, not arbitrary.

Naboth was obedient to the laws I gave Israel. He understood the importance of keeping the land he had inherited—the land I had given his ancestors—even when the king sought to purchase it. The cost of obedience was great, but my servant stood firm for what he knew was right.

You'll meet plenty of people in life who only want what they want, without regard for me. But take heart—Scripture is full of faithful ones like Naboth who honored their commitment to me without fail and without regret.

I understand that it isn't always easy to do what is right, to stand against the crowd, to turn away from something lucrative because it is wrong. But I will honor you for your obedience. Stand strong!

Read
1 Kings 21:1–16.

Lord, I will do as you have asked, for your words are true.

APRIL 22

I see that Ahab is now sorry for what he has done. So I will not cause the trouble to come to him during his life. —
1 Kings 21:29 (NCV)

HOW MUCH

Child, you know I've seen what you have done, and you feel I could not forgive you, let alone love you. But you are wrong, my child. Nothing you could ever do would stop me from loving you. Nothing you have ever done is beyond the reach of my forgiveness.

King Ahab found this out firsthand. He sinned in the vilest of ways, but when confronted, he humbled himself before me. I in turn withheld his punishment.

At first you may not think he deserved to be forgiven—but I long to show my compassion to anyone who comes to me in repentance. Without exception. That's how much I love you.

When you fail, come to me and confess what you have done. Don't be ashamed to express your sorrow—I will have mercy. I will forgive.

Draw close to me and let me show you just how much I love you.

Read
1 Kings 21:17–29.

Lord, I come today to repent of my sins and to find your mercy.

*Elisha replied, "As surely as the
LORD lives and you yourself live,
I will never leave you." So they
went on together.*

—**2 Kings 2:6** (NLT)

MOMENT BY MOMENT

I love to see true commitment from my children. And I
appreciate it when they know they need me in order
to complete the tasks I have for them.

Elisha wanted to learn as much as he could from
my servant Elijah, so he remained at the prophet's side,
an eager and steadfast apprentice. Before I took Elijah
straight to heaven in a chariot of fire, Elisha even boldly
asked for a double share of the spirit Elijah had—longing
to serve as his mentor had served, wanting to glorify me
as Elijah did. I chose to answer his request just as boldly.

Let Elisha's experience be a reminder to you: I'm not
expecting you to figure things out on your own, to go in
your own strength. I know you need me and my Spirit to
do all that I have called you to do. Ask me—moment my
moment, day by day. I never tire of hearing from you.

Read
2 Kings 2:1–14.

*Father, I need you
every moment. May I
always remember to
call on you.*

*The company of the prophets
from Jericho, who were watching,
said, "The spirit of Elijah is
resting on Elisha."*

—2 Kings 2:15 (NIV)

LEGACY

You are part of a long line of believers across the centuries who have lived—and sometimes died—to share my message. From age to age, I have empowered my people to continue in that calling, by my Spirit. In your generation, I have poured out my Spirit on you. The same Spirit that filled Elisha fills you.

So, my child, what do people see when they look at you? My intent is that they recognize my Spirit in you, just as the prophets from Jericho recognized Elijah's spirit newly resting on Elisha.

When I call one of my servants to heaven with me, I always leave a legacy—someone who will follow behind and continue the work. Like Elisha for Elijah, like Timothy for Paul, like you for . . .

My spirit will help you continue the work my servants have been doing across the centuries. Join the task. We have much to do.

Read
2 Kings 2:15–25.

*Lord, as I go out into
the world, let your
Spirit rest on me.*

Naaman went down to the
Jordan River and dipped himself
seven times, as the man of God
had instructed him. —
2 Kings 5:14 (NLT)

NO MATTER WHAT

My mercy and compassion are for everyone. Sometimes people question this—in their own prejudices or preconceptions they attempt to put me in a box. But, beloved, I don't fit in any box.

Naaman was commander of an enemy army. In fact, bands of his men had taken some of the Israelites captive. One of my children, a young girl, ended up in the service of Naaman's wife. That daughter of mine could have been angry and decided that my love didn't apply to her captors. Instead, she decided to introduce them to me. When Naaman submitted to my command through my servant Elisha, I healed him.

I know where you are right now, my child—and I know who the "unreachables" are in your relationship circle. You have a difficult marriage, a surly employer, a ministry to those who don't seem to be listening . . . My love is for each of those people too. I want to reach them through you.

Read
2 Kings 5:1–18.

Lord, help me to be
your servant in even
my difficult situations.

*Joash was seven years old when
he began to reign.*   —
2 Kings 11:21 (NIV)

COME AND SERVE

Beloved, though your heart aches to hear me, when I
speak you sometimes wonder, *Can this really be God
calling me? Am I really able to do as he asks?*

My calls are not limited to the strong, the wise, the
successful, or the wealthy. My service is not restricted to
the age-appropriate few. My message and my ministry
are for all. A child who shares her lunch, a young adult
who helps his neighbor, an elderly person who shares his
wisdom—all are my servants. Joash was only seven when
he became king, and yet I called him, prepared the way,
and gave him advisers who would help him.

You're not too young, too old, too weak, too anything.
You are just as I created you. And I'm calling you to come
and serve.

Won't you join me?

Read
2 Kings 11.

*God, I'm listening.
No excuses. I want to
serve you.*

The king stood by the pillar and made a covenant in the presence of the LORD to follow the LORD and to keep His commandments.
—**2 Kings 23:3** (HCSB)

JUST FOR YOU

Dear child, you can find my promises, my desires, my expectations, and my love expressed in my Word. I am the God who does not change, and my words have not changed. They are the same today as when they were first written–giving light in the darkness, life to the lifeless, and hope to the hopeless.

For many years my people Israel forgot me and all I'd said. The temple door was nailed shut and the book that held my laws had been buried. When the book was finally rediscovered and read, King Josiah recognized how far the people had strayed and he revived a spirit of obedience to my decrees.

You are fortunate to have a copy of my Word that you can read every day. Your Bible holds my words for all of life. Read it and see: the covenants I have made; the commands I have spoken; the truths I have shared. Each utterance has been lovingly offered up and unerringly delivered, just for you.

Read
2 Kings 22:1–13;
23:1–3.

Lord, yours are the words of eternal life. I will write them in my heart.

APRIL 28

With praise and thanks, they sang this song to the LORD: "He is so good! His faithful love for Israel endures forever!"
—**Ezra 3:11** (NLT)

BUILD WISELY

From the beginning I have loved you. And in my love for you, I willingly provide for all your needs. I do this because you are my child and I want to have a relationship with you.

In meeting your needs, I have also given you the words of life—tools to help you build a foundation in me. Take a lesson from those who rebuilt the temple in Ezra's day: build wisely. Start by building on what you know to be true of me. Soak in my faithfulness and grace. Believe that I am holy and just. Know that no matter what may come your way, my love for you does not run out.

With this solid foundation, you can withstand the storms of life.

Read
Ezra 3.

Lord, you have given me the tools I need to build my life in you.

The king said to me, "What is it you want?" Then I prayed to the God of heaven. —
Nehemiah 2:4–5 (NIV)

COMPELLED TO THE CALL

I never call you without equipping you. Sometimes my call entails burdening your heart over a need you see in your world. Nehemiah felt great sadness that the walls of my city, Jerusalem, still lay in ruins. And though he was in a faraway land, serving another nation's king, he sensed that his sorrow had a purpose—he sensed that I had a task for him and that I would open the way for him to do it. Thus compelled to action, Nehemiah made his requests known; he did not shy away from seeking my help and then asking the king for his. And the king and I both poured out our favor on him.

My resources are limitless for your task. Voice prayers to me whenever you have a question, a concern, or just need assurance that I'm there. I will provide, seeing to it that you have everything you need.

Read
Nehemiah 2:1–10.

I sense a need, Lord, and my heart hurts. Show me what I can do.

APRIL 30

*Our enemies ... realized that
this work had been done with
the help of our God.* —
Nehemiah 6:16 (NIV)

MISSION IMPOSSIBLE?

It looked like an impossible task. The wall around
Jerusalem had been broken down and burned. The
stones were heavy. The work was tiring. And the enemies
in the land were not happy that my people had returned
to rebuild the wall and their lives. Those enemies did
everything they could to stop the work.

It's really no different in your world, dear one.
I know that sometimes when you try to do "mission
impossible" for me, people throw all kinds of things your
way to discourage you. But just as Nehemiah stayed on
task, acted wisely, and continually sought my guidance, so
can you.

Don't get discouraged. I have called you and I will
accomplish it. Like Israel, whose "impossible" task was
completed in fifty-two days, everyone will look at you and
know that the work was done with the help of your God.

Read
Nehemiah 6:1–16.

*Lord, I can do all
things because you give
me strength.*

MAY

MAY 1

[Ezra] read [God's Law] aloud from daybreak till noon ... in the presence of the men, women and others who could understand. —**Nehemiah 8:3** (NIV)

MY WORDS ARE TRUTH

When Ezra stood and read my words to my people, I was delighted. I loved their careful attention and resolve to hide my words in their hearts. I blessed that resolve with a move of my Spirit.

Child, I am just as delighted when you spend time soaking up my truths. In the busyness of this day, even if you cannot take large amounts of time in the Word, give me at least a few minutes. Then I can sprinkle your mind with seeds of comfort and peace to carry you through your day.

My dearest child, look for me in my Word. You will always find me there.

Read Nehemiah 8.

Lord, thank you for the truth of your Word.

MAY 2

*Let the king give [Queen Vashti's]
royal position to someone else
who is better than she.*

—**Esther 1:19** (NIV)

ALL THE RIGHT PIECES

Beloved, my plans for you have been in place since the foundations of the earth. And my plans always come to pass.

I worked through the troubles of the king and queen of Persia to open the way for my servant Esther to be in the royal court. No one knew what was soon to befall my people, but I did. I desired to have one of my children in a position of influence with the king.

My ways are not always clear, so when strange things seem to happen in your world, trust that I have a plan and I am moving circumstances in that direction. What looks confusing to you is simply me putting the right pieces in place for the next part of my plan.

Your part? Just continue walking daily with me. You never know when I will call you to a task larger than yourself.

Read
Esther 1.

*I will walk with
you, Lord, and be
ready whenever and
wherever you need me.*

*Hadassah . . . was also called
Esther. When her father and
mother died, Mordecai adopted
her into his family.*
—**Esther 2:7** (NLT)

OPEN OPPORTUNITIES

Dear child, I see the hardships you have endured, the many tears you have cried. Even when you don't sense my presence, I am right there with you, directing your steps.

You view your difficulties as closed doors, but your vision is clouded by pain. Blink away your tears, lift up your head, and look again. Closed doors are actually open opportunities for you to experience my compassion and grace.

Though Esther experienced the loss of her parents, I still had special plans for her, just as I have for you. In the midst of your trials, stay close to my side, sheltered in my protection. My perfect love, paired with your humbled heart, will draw others to me. And together, we will do amazing things to advance my kingdom.

Read
Esther 2:1–18.

*Help me to approach
every difficulty with
a soft heart and a
teachable spirit.*

*Mordecai would not bow down
or show [Haman] honor.*
—**Esther 3:2** (NCV)

SET APART

When my people take a stand for me, I stand with them. When they honor me before others, I honor them. Though Mordecai suffered the scorn of a powerful man in the kingdom, I raised him to greatness because of his trust in me.

Child, I am mindful of the times when you feel alone in the struggle to honor me—not all of your contemporaries value righteous living, do they? But don't give up. Keep running the race anyway.

The course I set before you is indeed lonely at times. Nevertheless, I have set you apart and equipped you to run it well. I have also prepared your path with rich blessings and rewards. So take courage, and know that when you feel like you're standing alone, you aren't. I am standing with you.

Read
Esther 3.

*Lord, grant me the
courage to stand for
you every day, in every
situation.*

Who knows if perhaps you were made queen for just such a time as this? —**Esther 4:14** (NLT)

FOR SUCH A TIME AS THIS

I am the God of all times and all circumstances. I set my servants in place throughout the ages, at just the right times, in order to usher in change, hope, or deliverance.

I established you where you are today, my child. *You* are the one I have called to this time, this place, this situation. I also know your fears. Like Esther, you wonder how effective you can be and you fear the results of stepping out in faith.

Just trust me, dear one. Think back over our life together. Remember the promises I've kept. Recall the times of peace and provision, my faithfulness and goodness. With me, you can do all things.

Rest in that knowledge and the assurance that I have called you to such a time as this. Put your trust in me, for your times are in my hands.

Read
Esther 4.

I am your servant, Lord, for such a time as this.

When [the king] saw Queen Esther standing there in the inner court, he welcomed her and held out the gold scepter to her. —**Esther 5:2** (NLT)

YOU ARE WELCOME

E sther didn't know what would happen when she appeared before the king. She literally took her life into her hands to go to the king unbidden. But she knew this was the only way to save her people.

I am a different kind of King, loved one. You have an open invitation to come before me—anytime you like. I created you in hopes of a relationship. I long for you to willingly give me your heart.

So come. Any moment of the day or night. I am always here for you. See the scepter I extend toward you? It is the forgiveness and mercy paid for by my Son's blood. Like Xerxes' scepter, it allows you entrance to my throne room. Boldly approach. You are always welcome here.

In my presence you will find grace and mercy to help in your time of need.

Read Esther 5.

Thank you that I can come into your presence, Lord.

MAY 7

Haman has set up a sharpened pole that stands seventy-five feet tall. . . . He intended to use it to impale Mordecai. —
Esther 7:9 (NLT)

TREACHERY TO TRIUMPH

Fear not, beloved. I am well aware of the evil that exists in the world—and of those who try to hurt my people for their belief in me. And I will use their treachery to my advantage, to *your* advantage. Those who plot evil against you will find those plots used against them.

So don't fret. I have everything under control. When circumstances appear insurmountable, just remember: that's when I do my best work. I use the foolish to shame the wise, and choose the weak to shame the strong. And I will use the wicked to the advantage of the righteous.

Rest in my care and leave the details to me. I can turn treachery into triumph.

Read
Esther 7.

I praise you for protecting me even in the midst of evil.

MAY 8

The LORD said to Satan, "Where have you come from?" Satan answered the LORD, "From roaming through the earth."
—**Job 1:7** (NIV)

I HAVE OVERCOME

Dear one, your concerns about evil, pain, and loss in this world are valid. I've created you to care about such important issues! I care too. With all my heart.

Though plenty of people blame me for trouble or question why I allow suffering, the truth is that an enemy roams the earth, seeking to influence and destroy. Anytime you see deception, senseless violence, or unexplainable loss, he has a hand in it. At this time I have not yet banished all evil from the earth—so Satan still roams about. He wants to destroy you like he tried to destroy my servant Job.

Satan may be a formidable foe, and pain his ugly tool, but he is no match for me. As long as you remain close to me, you have nothing to fear.

Because I have overcome him, you can too. And one day I will banish all evil completely.

Read
Job 1.

Lord, open my eyes to Satan's deception, and keep my focus on you.

[Job's] wife said to him, "Are you still holding on to your integrity? Curse God and die!"
—**Job 2:9** (NIV)

BITTER OR BETTER?

My beloved child, your cries never go unnoticed. When you call out to me, I hear you and I respond. Although your pain may feel unbearable, you can trust that a better story is being written in your life.

Job understood that both good and evil happen to my people, yet I still love them. He also recognized that I am still and always God. Job's wife, on the other hand, felt that I had failed them both. Her bitterness did nothing to help Job, and it certainly did not help her either. I wish she had brought her pain to me.

How much better it is to simply trust me no matter what happens. You do not know the back-story; you do not see all of my plans or how I am working even now to redeem your pain. But when you trust me anyway, you acknowledge who I am and what I can do.

And that is so much better than being bitter.

Read Job 2.

In the middle of my pain, I can become bitter or better. Help me choose to be better.

Where were you when I laid the foundations of the earth? Tell Me, if you have understanding.
—**Job 38:4** (NKJV)

I AM YOUR GOD

My child, here is a truth to bring you some measure of relief from the pressure of your day: *you aren't God.* I say that because I want to take the burden off your shoulders. You don't have to make everything in your world work according to your plans. If you simply let go and rest in me, I'll take care to make everything work according to *my* plans.

My love for you is greater and deeper than you will ever understand. So are my wisdom and power. As with my servant Job, I welcome your questions, your sorrows, your requests, and—above all—your burdens. I will walk with you each day of your life, and through the difficult times in particular, because I love you. And because I am God. *Your* God.

Read
Job 38.

God, help me surrender control and allow you to guide me.

I have declared that which I
did not understand, things too
wonderful for me, which I did
not know. —**Job 42:3** (NASB)

SOME WONDERFUL TRUTHS

Beloved, I joyfully reveal myself to you in many ways.
When the birds sing in the morning, I sing to you
through them. When the trees gently wave in the breeze,
they call attention to my presence. When a baby smiles
at you, know that I am smiling too. Yet there are some
truths I keep beyond your grasp, and mysteries I choose
not to explain just yet.

I loved Job's humility, the fact that he could admit
that there were truths he didn't understand. When he
surrendered his "right to know," I rejoiced. And I blessed
him for his faith.

Child, when you're in pain and don't understand why,
will you trust me anyway? Trust that when life seems out
of control, it is never out of *my* control.

Read
Job 42.

God, help me to trust
that you're good and
that you know what
you're doing.

For the LORD watches over the path of the godly, but the path of the wicked leads to destruction.
—**Psalm 1:6** (NLT)

YOUR CHOICE

From the beginning I have loved you as my own. I have chosen you for a special purpose, provided for your needs, and comforted you in difficult times. I delight to do all of this. It is my joy to reveal the plans I have for you, to walk by your side, to see you through every challenge.

In fact, I love you so much that when I created you, I set within you the freedom of choice: to choose my path or other paths. I also offered you the wisdom to choose wisely.

I will not force you to take my path; but, oh my child, how I yearn for your love and trust! Won't you choose to take my hand and walk with me today?

Read
Psalm 1.

You are my God, and I choose to live in obedience to you.

You have made them a little lower than God, and crowned them with glory and honor.
—**Psalm 8:5** (NRSV)

MY DEEPEST SATISFACTION

With great joy I created the heavens and the earth, the moon and stars, the mountains and valleys, the rivers, oceans, and fields. Every atom in the universe bears my unique fingerprint. My deepest satisfaction, however, was in creating you.

You mean more than the world to me. That is why I have made you only a little lower than my heavenly creatures. That is why I crowned you with glory and honor and gave you dominion over the plants and animals.

How much are you worth? I sent my Son Jesus into the world to save you from your sins so we can enjoy eternity together. You are of infinite value to me.

Read
Psalm 8.

Lord, help me believe my great worth in your eyes.

The LORD is my shepherd;
I have all that I need.

—**Psalm 23:1** (NLT)

YOUR SHEPHERD

I am the Good Shepherd. I watch over you. I guide you along safe paths, across lush green pastures, to quiet waters where you can drink. I know when you need rest, and I lead you to peaceful places where you can gain new strength. When you need help, I am there. When you get lost, I come and find you. And when you walk through dark valleys, I'm right beside you, guarding, guiding, comforting.

My goodness and unfailing kindness will be with you all of your life, and afterwards you will live forever with me in my home.

When I am your Shepherd, you have everything you need!

Read
Psalm 23.

Heavenly Father, when
I have you, I have
everything I need.

Create in me a clean heart, O God, and renew a right spirit within me. —
Psalm 51:10 (ESV)

A CLEAN HEART

A heart longing to change always gets my attention, beloved. When David cried out to me to change his heart, my Spirit was already there, pouring out grace and mercy.

Come to me when you are in need of a clean heart. Don't be discouraged or embarrassed—I will not condemn you. Simply ask for my forgiveness and give me all the sinful and ugly things that have stained your soul. And when you do, I will wash you clean and give you a fresh start.

You're the joy of my heart. Why wouldn't I do everything within my power to restore my relationship with you?

Read
Psalm 51.

Lord, I offer you my sin and shame. Please wash me anew so I can be clean.

Where morning dawns and evening fades you call forth songs of joy. —**Psalm 65:8** (NIV)

SONGS OF JOY

The work of an artist always points back to its creator. Do you remember the last breathtaking sunset you watched? I shared it with you because I love you. The beauty you see in the sky, or the sea, or the forest, or across the plain—all of it points you to me. Every good thing in this world is designed to praise me. Even the rocks testify of my works.

Child, the witness of the world around you affirms that I love your worship in any form—your songs, your gratitude, your talents and treasures, even your stumbling words of praise and your sighs of amazement when words fail. In heaven's language, a sigh can be high praise when my Spirit inspires you.

Take time to look around, beloved. Let the beauty of my creation bring forth songs of joy from your heart and life!

Read
Psalm 65.

God, thank you for sharing yourself with me. You inspire me to praise you!

*Bless the LORD, O my soul, and
do not forget all his benefits.*
—**Psalm 103:2** (NRSV)

HAPPILY EVER AFTER

Most people long for a happily ever after—the kind
of life that fairy tales describe, where the prince
gets the true princess, evil is banished, and all is well.

I do offer a happily ever after. And it starts today.
When you let me write your story, I forgive your sins. I
heal you. I redeem your life. I crown you with love and
compassion. These are just some of my benefits. The list
goes on . . .

Look up at the sky. My love for you is higher than
that. Look east and then west. That is how far I've
removed your sins from you. Look around you. I am
always at work, bringing circumstances together for good,
and supplying you with my gracious gifts.

Finally, look within. I have given you my Spirit as
a guarantee that everything I have is yours: my peace,
forgiveness, love, joy.

My beloved child, my happily-ever-after story is true.
Let me help you make it yours.

Read
Psalm 103.

*God, help me remember
the benefits of inviting
you into my life.*

I praise you because I am fear-
fully and wonderfully made.
—**Psalm 139:14** (NIV)

WONDERFULLY MADE

Long before the earth was formed, I knew you. Even before the universe came into existence, I loved you. While I carefully knit you in your mother's womb, I whispered in your tiny ears, "You are mine." You are my creation, my delight, my joy. Everything about you is intentional. Your nose. Your eyes. Your intellect.

I know you better than you know yourself—your thoughts before you think them; your words before you speak them. Nothing surprises me about you because every day of your life was determined by me before you were born.

I think about you all the time. While you sleep, I am watching over you. When you awake, I am at your side, eager to spend time with you.

Invite me in, my child. I want to lead you in the way everlasting.

Read
Psalm 139.

God of all compassion,
thank you for your
watchful care over me.

Above all else, guard your heart,
for it is the wellspring of life.
—**Proverbs 4:23** (NIV)

GUARD YOUR HEART

How I love to watch you grow and take risks! As you're maturing, you want to stretch, test your wings, make decisions for yourself. You want to run ahead and experience new things that will add richness to your life. I understand all of these desires, child. But in the process, I want you to also grow in grace and faith, and in your knowledge of me.

So guard your heart, my child. Be wise, be careful, be pure. As you experience the exciting new things life has to offer, establish good boundaries around yourself. Resist temptation and draw near to me. Let my wisdom keep you safe.

I have given you promises and commands that will protect you. Write them on your heart and mind. They will nourish you, guide you, and keep you for all the days of your life.

Read
Proverbs 4:1–23.

Lord God, give me
wisdom so that I will
guard my heart.

Let your fountain be blessed, and take pleasure in the wife of your youth. —**Proverbs 5:18** (HCSB)

COMMIT TO COMMITMENT

True love slakes your thirst like a cold drink of water on a hot day. It satisfies, refreshes, and makes you feel alive. That's why a lifelong commitment in marriage is beautiful to me.

Even with a fulfilling marriage, the temptation to drink from another fountain still exists, because the enemy seeks always to destroy. But while the water may look satisfying, it's laced with poison, child. Tragedy follows those who drink from fountains other than their own: devastated spouses, damaged children, disappointed friends. Worst of all, unfaithfulness deadens your heart— toward me and in future relationships.

I have a much better way, my child. As the one who specializes in commitment, ask me to help you stay faithful—and I'll be faithful to do just that.

Read
Proverbs 5:1–19.

Lord, help me to be faithful to my spouse (or future spouse), and to you.

MAY 21

Remember also your Creator in the days of your youth, before the evil days come and the years draw near. —**Ecclesiastes 12:1** (ESV)

REMEMBER ME

I've heard your prayers and I know the desires of your heart. I see your hopes and dreams and your longing to live a meaningful life. I know you yearn for purpose and direction and significance. That's why I invite you to remember me in every stage of your life.

Come, join with me and let's enjoy this moment together. While it is still today, let's explore all that I have provided for you to experience.

Some people want to put me off until they are old and gray. But trust me, there are things I want to show you now that can't wait until later.

Don't just seize the day—seize hold of *me*. I can't wait to venture out with you today.

Read
Ecclesiastes 12.

Lord, I want to pursue you today. Help me to use my time wisely.

I am a man of unclean lips, and I live among a people of unclean lips, and my eyes have seen the King, the LORD Almighty.
—**Isaiah 6:5** (NIV)

I BRIDGED THE GAP

Even while my holiness demands a separation from sin and evil, my love looks for ways to rescue those caught in the trap. After all, I did not create the world to remain separated from my loved ones.

When a glimpse of my majesty caused Isaiah to recognize his unclean lips, I cleansed him and called him to lead others to me. Isaiah could not cleanse himself, could not bridge the gap. I had to do it for him . . . for you . . . for the world.

I spanned the gap between us with a cross. Gladly. Now sin no longer separates us. Now you are free to come to me directly, with confidence, knowing you will be greeted by love and welcomed with joy.

Read
Isaiah 6:1–8.

Thank you for bridging the gap between my sinful heart and your holy presence.

*He was crushed for our
iniquities; the punishment that
brought us peace was upon
him, and by his wounds we are
healed.* —**Isaiah 53:5 (NIV)**

HEALED BY MY WOUNDS

When Isaiah wrote this prophecy, he did not
understand the scope of what I would one day
do through my Son. But, beloved, this is how deeply I
love you. I sent Jesus to take the weight of sin. He was
afflicted and pierced. The punishment that would bring
peace and forgiveness to you landed with full force on
him.

When he took all sin upon him, I had to look away,
for my holiness could not tolerate the sight of evil.
Separated from me, my Son died. This was the weight
that he bore for you, child. It was the only way I could
rescue you; the only way I could bring you life and hope
and healing.

Go ahead and celebrate—you are free! Free indeed!

Read
Isaiah 53.

*Jesus, my heart breaks
under sin, but rejoices
in your salvation.*

You must go to everyone I send you to and say whatever I command you. Do not be afraid of them. —**Jeremiah 1:7–8** (NIV)

LET'S DO THIS TOGETHER

Beloved, I know the fear that creeps into your heart when I call you, the fear that the task is beyond your ability. You worry that I have somehow made a mistake by calling you. I know your unrest, your uncertainty, my child. Most of all, I know your potential. I am willing to keep working on the masterpiece that is you until you reach that potential.

The task may be challenging, but it is never impossible. Jeremiah had a tough job and faced many difficulties, yet I was always with him. You will encounter difficulty as well, but my power is greater than any problem that comes our way.

Lean into this challenge. Push ahead with the confidence that I am right beside you. We're in this together.

Read
Jeremiah 1:1–10.

You know me better than I know myself, O God. Guide me as I seek to walk with you.

MAY 25

*Take another scroll and write
on it all the words that were on
the first scroll, which Jehoiakim
king of Judah burned up.*

—**Jeremiah 36:28** (NIV)

MY WORD REMAINS

Jeremiah's experience with Jehoiakim is not new to me.
For millennia I have been ignored altogether, or cast to
one side so people could run after other gods. But in you,
my precious child, I see a difference. I see a sincere love
for my Word and a passion to hear what I have to say.

It delights my heart to watch you pore over my
love letters to you. You are seeing me for who I am, and
getting to know my heart for you, and it only makes us
closer.

Some of your peers want to dismiss me as irrelevant.
Others would love to see my Word silenced—even
destroyed. But don't let them deter you or dishearten you.
I am rock-solid, and my Word remains. Forever true.

No one and nothing can come between us.

Read
Jeremiah 36.

*Lord, please give me
a passion to follow
your commands and
treasure your promises.*

MAY 26

*My lord the king, these men
have acted wickedly in all that
they have done to Jeremiah the
prophet.* —**Jeremiah 38:9** (NASB)

STAND

You are my child, my special creation, and I love to
share this world with you. Sadly, while you and
I walk together in peace, there are many who oppose
me, just as men opposed my prophet Jeremiah. Those
adversaries will confront you, trying to drag you away or
sow doubt and fear into your heart. But because my love
is more powerful than their hate, nothing they do can
keep me from you. Nothing they say can ever diminish my
passion for you.

You are my child, adopted into my kingdom and
loved beyond measure. So stand tall, dear one, in the full
confidence that I am with you. Together, through the
power of my Holy Spirit, we will resist the evil forces of
this dark world—and love will stand in the end.

Read
Jeremiah 38:1–13.

*Give me strength to
stand against all that I
know to be wrong.*

I will put my Spirit inside
you, and you will come to life.
—**Ezekiel 37:14** (NCV)

MY BREATH BRINGS LIFE

S ometimes I seem far away, and you feel that everyone
has turned against you. Sometimes life beats you
down and you wonder if I care.

Beloved one, I am here. Right here. Ready to reveal
myself in the ways you need me most.

The searing heat of anxiety and suffering can make
you feel as spiritually dry as dust. But even in those
times, you can come to me for refreshment. When you
think all hope is lost and nothing could possibly change, I
am your oasis, eager to welcome you into my shelter and
fill you up again. Simply come to me.

When you do, I will bring new life to your dry bones.
Right here, from this dusty ground, I will bring forth
abundant new life. A river of water that will quench your
thirst.

Can you taste it? Come to me and drink deeply.
Hope once again.

Read
Ezekiel 37:1–14.

Father, send your Holy
Spirit and breathe new
life into my dry bones.

Daniel determined that he would not defile himself with the king's food or with the wine he drank.
—**Daniel 1:8** (HCSB)

A LINE IN THE SAND

I see the challenges you face each day—those friends who tempt you to pull away from me, the coworkers who encourage you to ignore company policy. I also notice and celebrate as you take a stand for me.

When my servant Daniel was taken into exile, few people would have blamed him if he'd bent some of the rules. He was in hostile territory, after all—maybe the old loyalties no longer applied.

But Daniel knew that, foreign land or not, I was with him. And so he stood up for me! He drew a line in the sand and refused to cross it, and even his enemies realized I was God.

Sometimes you wonder if drawing a line in the sand makes you look silly or weak. The good news? It doesn't. You actually grow stronger and more attractive every time you seek to honor me.

Read
Daniel 1:1–17.

Lord, empower me to be a faithful and obedient servant.

Daniel went to his house and informed his friends . . . that they might request compassion from the God of heaven. —**Daniel 2:17–18** (NASB)

BETTER TOGETHER

Our prayer time together is precious to me. When you set aside everything and turn your heart to me, I rejoice. Daniel made prayer a priority even as the world pressed in—and he saw how I empowered and equipped him. Without that time together, he could not have done what I needed him to do in the face of so much opposition.

You can't do it alone either, child. There are times when you need not just my encouragement but the fellowship and encouragement of other believers. Asking for help is no sign of weakness. Instead, it is a primary source of strength.

Seek me out, and bring your friends along. Carve out some time so you can share your needs and concerns. I can't wait to hear—and answer—your prayers. It is my delight to spend time with you.

Read
Daniel 2:1–23.

We come before you now, seeking your help in all things.

The God of heaven will set up
a kingdom that will never be
destroyed.

—**Daniel 2:44** (NIV)

A KINGDOM THAT WILL LAST

C hild, I see your grief as you wonder: *Will the*
circumstances of my life ever change? Will this pain
I'm experiencing last forever?

Daniel spoke rightly of me to King Nebuchadnezzar,
and his message offers hope for your situation as well:
though Nebuchadnezzar's reign would end, and others
would rise up to take his place, my kingdom would never
end. That means that in my forever kingdom, child, you
have a place that will never be taken from you. Where
I live, all grief is gone. No harm can happen. So when I
take you to live with me, you will never again experience
disappointment, loss, or pain.

Beloved, when fear whispers that life will always
look as it does now, remind yourself of my promise that
"this too shall pass," and then focus on what will truly last
forever: my Word, my kingdom, my love for you.

Read
Daniel 2:24–49.

Heavenly Father, I am
grateful for my place in
your kingdom.

If we are thrown into the blazing furnace, the God whom we serve is able to save us. —**Daniel 3:17** (NLT)

IN THE FIERY FURNACE

Beloved, when you pass through circumstances that threaten to drown you in pain . . . when you encounter the fires of doubt and grief . . . when you are persecuted for honoring my name, I will be with you.

My servants Shadrach, Meshach, and Abednego put their very lives on the line to worship me. They knew the consequences, but still they rejected the king and his rash demand to commit idolatry.

In this fallen world, fiery furnaces of all kinds await you, child. Will you follow me into them anyway? I promise to sustain you, no matter what.

Read Daniel 3.

Lord, I will follow you and fear no other.

JUNE

JUNE 1

There is a man in your kingdom who has the spirit of the holy gods in him. —**Daniel 5:11** (NIV)

A GOOD REPUTATION

People are watching you, my child. They know that you know me, and they wonder what that really means. They may not read a Bible, but they read you— your reactions to difficulty, your attitude toward others, your level of integrity. Your coworkers are watching how thoroughly you live what you profess. Your neighbors are studying whether your faith makes your home any different from theirs.

You see, you are building a reputation. My servant Daniel had served me well, and he was known as the man to go to when the nation's wise men could not discern my mysteries. People had been watching. They knew that Daniel knew me.

Does anyone see me in you?

Read
Daniel 5.

May I represent you well, Lord, and build a good reputation for you.

JUNE 2

He prayed three times a day, just as he had always done, giving thanks to his God.

—**Daniel 6:10** (NLT)

THE SPECIAL JOY OF PRAYER

Nothing kept Daniel from talking with me—not even the threat of ending up in a den of lions. In fact, when he heard about the law against praying, the first thing he did was to come to me and pray.

That's how I want it to be with us, beloved. When the going gets tough, make me the first place you come, not the last. When you're so excited you can hardly stand it, tell me. Yes, I already know how you feel and what you're facing, but it gives me special joy when we talk about it.

So go ahead. Throw open your windows, kneel down, and pour out your heart to me. I love you so much, and I'm waiting to talk with you.

Read
Daniel 6:1–23.

Today I will pray and lift high the name of the Lord.

JUNE 3

I will be faithful to you and make you mine, and you will finally know me as the LORD.
—**Hosea 2:20** (NLT)

MY TENDER LOVE

You are my beautiful bride. I describe you that way throughout my Word because the love I have for you is like the love of a bridegroom for his bride.

That's the picture I asked my servant Hosea to live out before my people. They had been unfaithful by worshiping other gods. I wanted them to know that I still loved them and would bring them back. So I told Hosea to marry a woman who would be unfaithful. Always, he showed her tender love—just as I do with you.

My beautiful bride, I love you—even when you turn away from me or do wrong; even when you feel you have failed me. If you are unfaithful to me, I will come and draw you back. If you turn away for a time, I will find you and bring you home.

You are mine.

**Read
Hosea 2:14 – 3:5.**

Thank you for always loving me.

JUNE 4

I will pour out my Spirit on all people. —Joel 2:28 (NIV)

POURED OUT

My Spirit is in you, my child. He is your Counselor, your Advocate, your Guide—sent to those who accept my Son's sacrifice for their sin and choose to follow me. My Spirit lives within you to help you follow. He comforts. He even helps you pray when you can't find the words.

I showed this beautiful picture to my servant Joel—the picture of a day when my Spirit would be poured out and my people would be empowered to do great things for me.

With my Spirit in you, we are one. Never forget the closeness we share, my child. My Spirit is always with you. Let that bring you great comfort and joy. Nothing can separate you from my love.

Read
Joel 2:12–32.

Thank you for your Holy Spirit who lives within me.

JUNE 5

*Hate evil and love what is good;
turn your courts into true halls
of justice.* —**Amos 5:15** (NLT)

REACH OUT

I n my love for justice, I long for my people to hate evil, love what is good, and stand up for the less fortunate. I want my people to care for the poor and the needy, the widowed and the orphaned—anyone who needs an advocate.

That's what I call you to do, beloved. You are my ambassador in this world—one I've appointed to reach out to those who can't help themselves, who works to see justice done. At times, people will choose wrong over right—they'll exploit and mistreat others for their own selfish purposes—but remember that I am still in control, and I still summon you to seek justice on behalf of the helpless.

It's a tall order, to be sure. The world is often an unjust place. That's why I've called you to be a light in the darkness. Let me help you shine.

**Read
Amos 5:4–15.**

Give me a compassionate heart to care for those in need.

*The LORD provided a great fish
to swallow Jonah, and Jonah was
inside the fish three days and
three nights.* —**Jonah 1:17** (NIV)

BLESSING IN DISGUISE

My precious, frustrated child, I'm here. I know you
don't understand why I have you where you are
right now. You are eager to be out serving me, but at the
moment you feel you're on hold, with nothing to do and
no real purpose.

Why not take a break, my child, and spend some
time with me? My prophet Jonah needed a literal change
of direction, and I provided it. During those three days
in the fish, he began to understand who he was and
who I am. And that time of waiting helped him get his
perspective back.

Your time of waiting is not necessarily punishment
for anything. But you have been running from activity to
activity, with barely any time to think or talk. Use this
downtime to regain your perspective. It's my gift to you, a
blessing in disguise.

Read
Jonah 1.

*I will rest with you,
Lord. Help to correct
my perspective.*

JUNE 7

*In my distress I called to the
LORD, and he answered me.*
—**Jonah 2:2** (NIV)

CRY OUT TO ME

I could have given up on Jonah. I could have let him drown in the sea for trying to run from me. But I loved Jonah, and I still had work for him to do. So rather than choosing someone else to take my message to Nineveh, I persevered with him, determined to see him through.

I have called you, my precious one—and I will always find a way to bring you back to your calling. If you are on the run, cry out to me in the depths of your despair. Even when you think your situation is hopeless, I will hear you in your distress. I will answer. I will rescue.

You see, I'm not finished with you yet.

**Read
Jonah 2.**

*Thank you, Father, for
always hearing me.*

Nineveh has more than 120,000 people living in spiritual darkness.... Shouldn't I feel sorry for such a great city?

—Jonah 4:11 (NIV)

COMPASSION FOR THE LOST

When the people of Nineveh turned from their sin and repented, I was glad to show them mercy instead of judgment! What a wonderful day that was.

There was a time when you also walked in the ways of this world, stumbling in rebellion against me. But I remember the glorious moment when my salvation broke into your life and you received the first taste of my joy. That too was a wonderful day!

My compassion is for the lost, no matter how deep their darkness. I want them to choose me just as you did. So come on, let's share this free gift of new life with all who would take it. I desire that none should perish, but that all should come to repentance and enjoy eternal life with me—*with us.*

Read
Jonah 3–4.

Help me to be a vessel of your grace in the middle of a broken world.

JUNE 9

A ruler of Israel will come from [Bethlehem]. . . . And he will be the source of peace.

—**Micah 5:2, 5** (NLT)

RAYS OF HOPE

When my people needed to hear my voice in a dark time, I sent Micah with a message: the promise of a coming Savior-King, and word of where he would be born. Many of my prophets spoke of him—he would bring justice and restoration, he would do miracles, and one day he would die to save the world from sin. Centuries later, Micah's words would direct the wise men to Bethlehem, and to restored hope for my people.

Let that moment in history remind you today that even in the darkest times, I don't forget you—I promise a ray of hope. Even when my words are hard to hear—asking you to make some changes, showing you where there is still work to do in your life—you can trust that I'll give you the promises of my love, my faithfulness, my peace to see you through.

Those promises are meant to remind you of how much I care.

Read Micah 5:1–5.

Father, may I hear all your words—the tough ones as well as the great promises.

*What does the L*ORD *require of you? To act justly and to love mercy and to walk humbly with your God.* —**Micah 6:8** (NIV)

WALK WITH ME

Walking with me is not a complex endeavor, my child. Many people claim that I make too many rules, or that I require too much of them. But what do I require of my children? I made it clear through my prophet Micah.

I desire that my people act justly toward others—being fair, honest, filled with integrity. That they love mercy and pass it along to everyone they meet. And that they simply walk with me, in humility and thankfulness for all I have done.

When my Son came, he said it another way: he told his listeners to love me with all their heart, soul, mind, and strength, and to love their neighbors as themselves. Different words, same message.

Love me. Love others. Not complicated at all.

Read
Micah 6:1-8.

Teach me to do justly, to love mercy, and to walk humbly with you.

JUNE 11

The LORD is good, a refuge in times of trouble. He cares for those who trust in him.

—**Nahum 1:7** (NIV)

YOUR REFUGE

Rest in this promise: I made you with care, I watch over you with a keen eye, and I am an ever-present protection when you are afraid.

Just as when Israel was threatened by the powers of Assyria, so in these days of terrorism, fear, and economic threat, you too can trust in the truth that I am good. That I am your refuge in times of trouble.

You are quick to try and dodge every threat that surrounds you. To take matters into your own hands. But instead of getting caught up in desperation, let yourself experience my presence, my goodness, my faithfulness, my steadfast love. Take refuge in my protective embrace. That is where you will find rest for your soul.

Read Nahum 1. | *I will not run today; I will rest in the refuge you have prepared for me.*

For the earth will be filled with the knowledge of the glory of the LORD, as the waters cover the sea.
—**Habakkuk 2:14** (NIV)

KNOWING ME

Ask me your questions, beloved one. The small questions that rustle in your mind. The big ones that keep you awake at night. The deep ones with hurt and pain attached that cause you to doubt me. I promise to hear every concern.

My servant Habakkuk didn't understand my ways, so he asked his questions and then waited for my answers. And I gave them. He still didn't completely understand, but he knew he could trust me. He understood that all of eternity is in my hands.

One day, you will understand completely. One day I will make myself fully known. Until then, ask away. I will answer as much as you can understand.

Read
Habakkuk 2.

I have some questions for you, Lord. Thank you for hearing me.

JUNE 13

*The Sovereign LORD is my
strength; he makes my feet like
the feet of a deer, he enables me
to go on the heights.*

—**Habakkuk 3:19** (NIV)

LIVE THE ADVENTURE

My child, when I said I came to bring life to
the fullest, I meant it. In your adventure with
me, every situation has purpose. Every encounter has
meaning. Every day has opportunity for you to move
forward on the path I have laid out for you.

I will be your strength and your reason for rejoicing
at every step of your journey—leading you through green
pastures, giving you rest beside still waters. When you
walk through the valley of the shadow of death, I will
comfort you. When the trees don't bud, and the crop fails,
and your possessions are gone, I will not fail or leave you.
And when you are called to the heights, I will make your
feet sure and your legs strong.

Let's live the adventure together!

Read
Habakkuk 3.

*Make my feet like the
feet of a deer. Enable
me to go on the heights!*

JUNE 14

The LORD your God ... will
take great delight in you, he will
quiet you with his love, he will
rejoice over you with singing.
—**Zephaniah 3:17** (NIV)

PURE DELIGHT

I t is my joy to send you special gifts—your family, the
sunshine streaming through your windows, that ice
cream sundae, the scent of lilacs, the feeling of the wind in
your face as you exercise. Those things give you a special
contentment. But it goes even deeper. They bring a smile
to your face. They delight you and bring you joy!

That's how I feel when I look at you. Sheer delight.
Unbounded pleasure. I can't help but smile, for you are
my special creation. My love rains down on you like a
summer shower. I quiet your fears and worries with my
love. I rejoice over you in song.

You delight me, my child. You are wonderful,
beautiful. You give me joy.

R e a d
Z e p h a n i a h
3 : 8 – 2 0 .

I am amazed that you
delight in me! May I
always bring you joy!

JUNE 15

Now this is what the LORD Almighty says: "Give careful thought to your ways."

—**Haggai 1:5** (NIV)

RIGHT PRIORITIES

I see you busy with many good things. You are working so hard, yet you are tired and on your way to burning out.

Let's talk priorities, my dear one. I long to be first in your life—not just for my glory, but for your protection. I have tasks for you; I have tasks for others. I don't expect you to say yes to everything you're asked to do, but you'll only know my plans for you if you talk to me first. So let's take time together, today and every day, to talk things through.

Haggai had to talk to my people about their priorities. I want to talk with you about yours so you can be fulfilled in your tasks. When you put me and my plans first, everything else will fall into place.

Read
Haggai 1:1 — 2:9.

Give me guidance to know the tasks you have for me today, Lord.

JUNE 16

I am the Lord All-Powerful. So don't depend on your own power or strength, but on my Spirit.
—**Zechariah 4:6** (CEV)

MY STRENGTH, MY SPIRIT

Sometimes in this difficult world, you just need a good, strong, helping hand to keep you going. And that is what I am holding out to you.

In your weariness, be comforted: I am the Lord All-Powerful; I don't expect you to stay the course on your own strength. I assured Zerubbabel of this when I charged him with rebuilding my temple in Jerusalem. So I say it to you about the work you have today: Do not depend on your own power or strength. Instead, depend on my Spirit within you. I will give you the resources you need to keep going, the peace that you are in my will, and the hope and vision to complete the work.

My Spirit is in you, my child. That is all you need.

Read
Zechariah 4.

Help me not to depend on my strength, but on your Spirit in me.

JUNE 17

See if I will not open the flood-gates of heaven and pour out a blessing for you without measure.
—**Malachi 3:10** (HCSB)

BLESSING WITHOUT MEASURE

I long to bless you, to pour out my abundance upon you. I have more spiritual riches than you can imagine, and when I open the floodgates of heaven, blessings will pour out upon you without measure. I only ask that you trust me, my child. Trust that I know your every need and will meet it.

Every time you give back to me a portion of what you've been given, you affirm your understanding that everything comes from my hand. I don't need your tithes and offerings—the world and its treasures are already mine. But I ask you to give so that you have the joy of helping others and continuing my work in the world. And I want you to have the constant reminder that not only do I give without measure, but my love is without measure as well.

Read
Malachi 3:6 — 4:6.

Father, I give to you from the abundance that you have given to me.

JUNE 18

On coming to the house, [the wise men] saw the child with his mother Mary, and they bowed down and worshiped him.
—**Matthew 2:11** (NIV)

A GIVING HEART

The star in the sky brought the wise men to my Son's cradle. Their gifts, odd as they may seem to you now, were perfect gifts for this baby—perfect gifts for a King. And beyond the gold, frankincense, and myrrh, the best gift of all was their worship. The wise men came seeking a king. When they arrived at the manger, they knew immediately that this child was the King they sought. And they bowed and worshiped.

I long for you to come to me with all your needs, but I also long for you to come and just worship. Will you do it today? Take time to focus on my greatness. Sit in awe of who I am and what I have done for you. Behold my majesty.

You can start by thinking about that baby in the manger.

Read
Matthew 2:1–12.

Father, I stand in awe of you.

JUNE 19

So was fulfilled what the Lord had said through the prophet: "Out of Egypt I called my son."
—**Matthew 2:15** (NIV)

ALL IS WELL

My child, of this you can be sure: everything has a purpose. No event comes into your life without first passing through my hands.

During my Son's life on earth, every event had a purpose as well: to fulfill the prophecies and promises I had given to my people. King Herod thought he could prevent my kingdom from being established on this earth, but nothing would stop my plans. Neither could anything stop my Son from fulfilling his purpose.

And nothing will prevent my plans for you, beloved. Your world may rage and threaten, but don't despair; all is well. My purpose will stand.

Read
Matthew 2:13–23.

Lord, remind me, even in the tough times, that you have a purpose for me.

JUNE 20

Blessed are the poor in spirit, for
theirs is the kingdom of heaven.
—**Matthew 5:3** (NKJV)

BLESSED

I love to bless you, my precious one. I long to give you a life that overflows with joy, with fulfillment, with complete and utter blessing. But sometimes my teachings seem like contradictions, don't they? Like when I use the words *poor* and *kingdom, mourn* and *comforted, hunger* and *filled* in the same sentence. *How can one be blessed by being poor, by mourning, by being hungry?* you ask. *How can persecution be a benefit?*

The world tells you the opposite is true—that my only blessings are affluence, ease, success. But that's what makes life with me so amazing: I turn the world's wisdom upside-down.

Put your faith in me, not in anything the world can offer you. Let me bless you with what really brings true joy, true fulfillment, true peace.

Read
Matthew 5:1–16.

Father, thank you for
the blessedness of my
life with you.

JUNE 21

*Love your enemies! Pray
for those who persecute you!*
—**Matthew 5:44** (NLT)

YOU SHOW THAT YOU'RE MINE

A s my child, you stand out in the world. Anytime you
act in ways that are contrary to the world's ways,
you make an instant impression. When you refuse to
retaliate when you've been wronged, but instead respond
with kindness, people take notice. When you forgive
someone who has hurt you, when you pray for those who
persecute you, when you love your enemies, you show
that you are mine.

I know it isn't easy, precious one. Sometimes you feel
taken advantage of and want to strike back; sometimes
you simply want to see justice done. I understand. But all
the more, that's when you need to wait on me. At times
I will ask you to leave justice in my hands, and at times
I will guide you to act to obtain the world's justice. But
that's the point: let *me* guide you.

After all, many are watching. And I want them to see
me in you.

Read
Matthew
5:31–48.

*Lord, it's hard to
love those who have
hurt me. I need your
assistance.*

JUNE 22

Give your gifts in private, and
your Father, who sees everything,
will reward you.

—**Matthew 6:4** (NLT)

AUDIENCE OF ONE

Dear one, don't worry. I see what is done in secret,
and I remember every faithful act. I am your
audience of one.

Sometimes you wish others would notice too; it's
natural to want to be praised. But don't get caught up in
the desire for recognition. People don't see what I see, and
they don't value what I value. Truly, it is your heart that
is most important to me.

No matter how small your gift seems, or how little
you think you have to give, you serve me well when you
give your all, quietly.

After all, I am watching. And I don't miss a thing.
Especially when you act in my name.

Read
Matthew 6:1–18.

Lord, I'm glad you are
watching over me.

JUNE 23

You cannot be the slave of two masters!... You cannot serve both God and money.

—**Matthew 6:24** (CEV)

YOUR ONLY MASTER

Oh my dear child, I understand how difficult the issue of money is in your world. You must have money in order to function, to simply survive—and yet I tell you not to be mastered by it.

It's a fine line that I ask you to walk, but because I want the best for you, I ask it anyway. Why? Money is a harsh and difficult master that is never satisfied. Money never lets you rest, never gives you peace or contentment. It always wants more. If you give yourself to it, money will take your world and every ounce of joy, as well as robbing you of your sensitivity to others.

Let me be your only Master. When you serve me with your money—using it wisely, holding it loosely, giving it freely—you are free. Free to see what we can do in the world!

Read
Matthew
6:19 – 34.

Let me be your servant, Lord. Keep me from being enslaved to money.

JUNE 24

Judge not, that you be not judged.
—**Matthew 7:1** (NKJV)

FOR THE RIGHT REASONS

*J*udge not. So many people take these words the wrong way, convinced that those who follow me should be accepting and tolerant of everything—even sinful things.

My child, when you hear such attitudes, remind yourself that I have asked you to strive for something the world does not understand: holiness. I want you to stand out, to stand strong—and at times to stand against evil—but for the right reasons. So the issue is not for you to bend over backward to accept anything in the name of tolerance; the issue is for you to be discerning and loving in all your ways, in honor of my holy name.

Judgment belongs to me and me alone. Wisdom and discernment are what I give you so that you can humbly present my truths and yet speak for me in love. When your words are seasoned with my grace rather than judgment, just watch—I will use your words to draw people to me.

Read Matthew 7:1–12.

Lord, give me discernment and wisdom to speak for you.

JUNE 25

Everyone who hears these words of Mine and acts on them will be like a sensible man who built his house on the rock.

—**Matthew 7:24** (HCSB)

UNSHAKABLE

When my Son described the best way to build a life, he focused on the first rule of construction—start with a solid foundation.

To build a house on sand leaves a person with nothing but a pile of rubble after the rain and wind have passed through. In the same way, the person who hears what I have to say but refuses to do anything with those truths will eventually see his or her foundations crumble during life's storms.

You, my child, show great wisdom when you hear my words and seek to apply them. With my teachings as the foundation of your life, you will be secure. Nothing will be able to shake you.

You have my word on it.

Read
Matthew 7:13–29.

Help me to build my life's solid foundation on your Word.

JUNE 26

The harvest is plentiful but the workers are few.

—**Matthew 9:37** (NIV)

MY HARVEST

My child, you know how much I love you. And I'm so glad you love me in return! But sometimes, when you are loved and content, it's easy to become complacent. I do want you to rest in me, but I also want your help in making my love known to others.

When my Son walked the earth, he saw so many people in need of my love. He observed their confusion, their helplessness, their aimless wandering—like sheep without a shepherd—and he responded with active compassion. Do you see them too?

You have the peace, the security that comes from knowing me. Won't you share that with someone whose life needs my healing touch? The harvest is plentiful but the workers are few. Will you be one of my workers?

Read
Matthew
9:27–38.

Dear Father, help me to recognize those around me who need to experience your love.

JUNE 27

Everyone who acknowledges me publicly here on earth, I will also acknowledge before my Father in heaven.

—**Matthew 10:32** (NLT)

HOLD FAST TO ME

I love you so much that I know exactly how many hairs are on your head. You are more valuable to me than anything else in my creation! So it grieves me when you are persecuted for loving me. But take heart, child: my Son meant it when he promised to unflinchingly acknowledge in heaven anyone who would call him theirs on earth.

I gladly reward such devotion with even greater devotion and faithfulness. No matter how difficult your road becomes, precious one, I will not leave you to walk it alone. I will give you the words to say precisely when you need them. I will empower you to acknowledge me even when it would be easier to stay silent.

In this world full of betrayals, I stand closer than a brother. Do not be afraid. I will never leave you or forsake you. Hold fast to me.

Read
Matthew
10:16–33.

Thank you, Lord, for so willingly calling me your own.

JUNE 28

Are you the Messiah we've been expecting, or should we keep looking for someone else?
—**Matthew 11:3** (NLT)

BRING YOUR QUESTIONS TO ME

Do you have questions? Bring them to me. The answers are waiting for you in my Word.

John the Baptist wasn't afraid to ask if my Son was truly the Messiah. Jesus answered him with the Scriptures as proof, pointing to how he was fulfilling the prophecies. And John understood.

Whenever you have doubts, come straight to me. Test new teachings against my Word. I have provided it for you, dear one, so that you may not be swayed by every wind of teaching but only by what is true.

As you devote yourself to my Word and to prayer, I will speak to you. As you grow in your understanding, I will give you insights into my will. Then no one will be able to draw you away from me. My truths will be your compass.

Read
Matthew 11:1–15.

Lord, help me to listen to your word that I may find the answers I seek.

JUNE 29

Anyone who isn't with me opposes me, and anyone who isn't working with me is actually working against me..

—**Matthew 12:30** (NLT)

ARE YOU WITH ME?

I don't want any of my children to be like the Pharisees. They claimed to be my servants, yet they rejected the abundant life my Son was offering and worked to deny his grace.

You, however, are very clearly mine. You came to me stained with sin's darkness, and I washed you whiter than snow. You now bear the fruit of a life rooted in me—good fruit that others can see. The treasury of your heart is full of grace and good things because you are with me, not against me.

Thank you for standing in one accord with me, for not causing division within my family. You are a blessing to others and to me.

Read
Matthew 12:22–37.

Lord, I am with you. Thank you for being in my life and helping me to bear good fruit.

JUNE 30

The Kingdom of Heaven is like a
treasure that a man discovered
hidden in a field.

—**Matthew 13:44** (NLT)

MY TREASURE

My kingdom is more valuable than anything
you could have or own. That's what Jesus was
illustrating when he told the parables of the man who
found the treasure in the field and the merchant who came
upon an exquisite pearl.

When you know the value of something, you're
willing to pay anything to have it. So it is with my
kingdom. Nothing you give up can begin to compare
to all that I have stored up for you. My blessings are
incalculable, unending, unimaginable.

No price is too high. After all, the cost I paid was
not measured in gold, but in blood. My only Son shed
his blood so that you, my precious child, could have that
treasure forever.

Read
Matthew
13:44–52.

Father, thank you for
offering your kingdom
to me as a gift. Help me
to recognize its value.

JULY

JULY 1

"But we have only five loaves of bread and two fish!" they answered. "Bring them here," [Jesus] said.

—**Matthew 14:17–18** (NLT)

WHAT DO YOU HAVE TO OFFER?

No one is so insignificant that I cannot use him or her to do great things. *No one.* If you think that your gifts are useless or inconsequential, remember that I designed you just the way you are—and I love you just the way you are. So give me what is in your hands and see what I will do.

I am the God who exponentially multiplied a few loaves and fish to feed thousands of people, with leftovers! There's no doubt that I can use your offerings—your pennies, your simple acts of service—to further the work of my kingdom.

Allow me to help you grow in faith, and in your willingness to use the gifts you have been given.

Read
Matthew
14:13–21.

Father, take me and use me. I am willing to help further your kingdom.

Jesus immediately said to them:
"Take courage! It is I. Don't be
afraid." —**Matthew 14:27** (NIV)

DO NOT BE AFRAID

Long ago, in the midst of a storm, my servant Peter believed that my power would enable him to walk on water. And he did—until he took his eyes off of me. That is when fear of the storm overwhelmed him, and he began to sink.

In the worst of life's storms, the sand shifts beneath your feet, the lightning flashes around you, and the undertow threatens to pull you down. But you can take courage, dear child, because I am here! I will never let you get pulled under.

With my power, you can handle the storms. Simply keep your eyes on me within the gale. My hands will deflect the lightning, and my voice will drown out the thunder. And as I do my work, your faith will become ever stronger, ever more stable in life's swirling tides.

Do not be afraid.

Read
Matthew
14:22–36.

Lord, help me to face
every storm with
courage, knowing that
you are always with
me.

JULY 3

So anyone who becomes as humble as this little child is the greatest in the Kingdom of Heaven. —**Matthew 18:4** (NLT)

IN THE FAMILY

Do you notice how I refer to you as my child? True, you have earthly parents, but when you humbled yourself in repentance and were reborn into my family, you became my child.

As your heavenly Father, I love you no matter what. But one of the best parts of being adopted by me is sharing in the inheritance of my Son. Think of it: Jesus is now both Savior and brother to you!

Your place in my family doesn't rest upon what you can do, how much wealth you accumulate, or how many friends you have. It comes from the simple act of kneeling at the cross. In that humility is true status—as my beloved child.

Read
Matthew
17:24 – 18:6.

Lord, remind me who I am in you—your precious child.

JULY 4

*It is not the will of my Father
who is in heaven that one of
these little ones should perish.*
—**Matthew 18:14** (ESV)

NONE SHOULD PERISH

My love for you is what brought my Son to the cross. He died so that you would have eternal life.

If only everyone on earth would come to me as you did: humble and repentant. It is not my will that any should be lost for eternity. I pursue lost souls just as a shepherd searches for his lost sheep. That is how I found you, my child. You were a lamb gone astray, crying out for help. I forgave you, restored you, and I now call you my own.

You are special to me! Thank you for accepting my love and returning it to me.

**Read
Matthew
18:10–20.**

*Thank you, Father,
for seeking me out
when I was lost—and
for loving me as your
very own child.*

JULY 5

The kingdom of heaven is like a landowner who went out early in the morning to hire workers for his vineyard.

—Matthew 20:1 (HCSB)

THE EYES OF GRACE

You sometimes wonder what heaven will be like. Let me assure you: it is beyond human language, child. Think of the loveliest spot you have ever seen on earth. My kingdom is far more beautiful. And its citizens are enjoying the perfection of an eternity with me.

Who will be there? You will, along with every other person who has accepted my Son as their Savior. Some will have spent a lifetime loving and serving me, while others will have come to me on their deathbed. There will be a few surprises too—certain people you didn't expect, but who softened their hearts in time to come to me.

You see, dear one, in the eyes of my grace, your future is promised whether you've known me for ninety years, or only two minutes. Every man, woman, or child who comes to me in the name of Jesus will enjoy my heaven and all its unspeakable riches—because my mercy is for everyone who asks.

Read
Matthew 20:1–19.

Lord, thank you for the promise of an eternity with you.

JULY 6

Hosanna to the Son of David!
"Blessed is He who comes in the
name of the LORD!"
—**Matthew 21:9** (NKJV)

AN EYE TO THE SKY

Beloved, one day I am coming back to take my people home with me!

I came the first time in the person of my Son. The people of Jerusalem knew a King was in their midst when Jesus entered the city riding on a donkey.

I will come again someday too. I know the exact moment when that glorious day will arrive—when my Son will win the final victory. But because no one on earth knows the time, I urge you to always be watching and ready.

While your heart longs for that day when we will finally be face to face, keep living your life, caring for your responsibilities, and using your gifts to serve me. But also keep an eye to the sky, my child. I'm coming soon.

Read
Matthew 21:1–17.

I am watching for your
return, Lord Jesus!

JULY 7

The stone which the builders rejected has become the chief cornerstone.

—**Matthew 21:42** (NKJV)

ALWAYS AND FOREVER MINE

Beloved, you are not alone. I know all about rejection. I face it every day as people choose to sin, choose their own way, choose other gods they think will get them where they want to go.

It hurts to work hard only to be passed over, to love only to be set aside. My Son was rejected by many he came to save. But man's opinion could not set aside my purposes; the rejected stone—my Son—became the cornerstone of a new house I was building: the household of faith. And you, my precious child, are a part of it.

Come to me and lay your hurts down. I will never reject you. You are mine.

Read
Matthew
21:28–46.

Thank you, Father, that I am yours, always and forever.

JULY 8

When the banquet was ready, he
sent his servants to notify those
who were invited. But they all
refused to come!

—**Matthew 22:3** (NLT)

WELCOME TO THE PARTY

I have a great party prepared! I constantly send out
invitations. My messengers follow up. But still, many
folks decide to decline.

My dear child, how happy I am that you have
accepted my invitation! Not only did you delight me
when you sent your RSVP, but the whole host of heaven
rejoiced.

The party will be the greatest celebration anyone
has ever seen. It will feature my Son as host, and we will
rejoice together that sin and death have been defeated.

Not everyone chooses to join in our fellowship, but
you, my precious child, have chosen to dine with me
forever. Welcome!

Read
Matthew 22:1–14.

Lord, thank you for
inviting me to join you
in sweet fellowship.

JULY 9

Well done.... You have been faithful in handling this small amount, so now I will give you many more responsibilities.
—**Matthew 25:21** (NLT)

KINGDOM WORK

Child, I have given you exactly what you need in order to do my kingdom work—the time, the abilities, the resources. You may not have as much as your friend, your neighbor, or even your spouse, but what's important is that you have *me*. And it is my joy to support and multiply your efforts.

Not only are you fully supplied, beloved, but no one else has been given your portion, your part. And no one else will feel as utterly fulfilled as you will when this unique work is done.

As you tend to what I've entrusted you with today, remember: I delight in helping you accomplish my work. And when it's finished, just like the king and his faithful servants, we will celebrate together.

Read
Matthew
25:14–30.

Dear Jesus, help me to use the resources I have wisely—to your glory, not mine.

JULY 10

*The King will reply, "I tell you
the truth, whatever you did for
one of the least of these brothers
of mine, you did for me."*
—**Matthew 25:40** (NIV)

HAVE A HEART

D ear one, do you realize love is a verb? It's true.
Out of my great love for you I redeemed you. And
through your kindness and compassion to others, you
extend my love and glorify me.

Cooking a hot meal, visiting the sick, donating
clothing, providing transportation for those who have
none—these small acts of mercy do not depend on great
amounts of wealth or even time. All that is needed is a
compassionate, responsive heart, and eyes to see the need
all around you.

If you ask me, I will gladly transform your heart to
be like mine: filled with compassion—a heart that seeks
and loves. When you show love and kindness to others,
you are showering me with love and kindness as well.

Read
Matthew
25:31–46.

*Lord Jesus, open
my eyes to the needs
around me. Open my
heart to love and serve
others.*

JULY 11

Peter said to all the people there that he was never with Jesus.
—**Mathew 26:70** (NCV)

NO FEAR

Beloved, I know why Peter denied my Son, and I know what tempts you to deny me too. From the silences when you should speak, to the witnessing opportunities you pass up because of what others might think, you are frequently besieged by fear.

When your faith feels like sinking sand, turn back to me, child. I am a Rock—your refuge in a time of need. I can forgive you and restore you, just as I did Peter. Ask for my strength, and for the courage to acknowledge me before others. I will enable you to speak up without shame, confident in your faith.

Read
Matthew
26:31–35, 69–74.

God, forgive me when I deny you in what I say—and in my silence. Strengthen my faith.

"I have sinned," [Judas] said, "for I have betrayed innocent blood." —**Matthew 27:4** (NIV)

NO REGRETS

My child, I long for you to live without the pain of regret. That's why I say in my Word to doubt your own understanding and rely on mine instead.

Only too late did Judas realize the consequences of ignoring my voice. When he tried to correct the situation, there was no going back; my Son was already in the hands of those who would kill him. It was a remorse that Judas couldn't live with—the kind of remorse that I don't ever want *you* to have to live with.

Beloved, this is a difficult lesson to learn. But much heartache and hurt can be avoided if you stop to consider the consequences of your decisions before you act. Talk to me first—and keep talking to me as you go. It is one move you will never regret.

Read
Matthew 27:1–10.

Dear Lord, give me the wisdom and guidance I need to make good decisions.

JULY 13

Tell the people that Jesus' followers came during the night and stole the body while you were asleep.
—**Matthew 28:13** (NCV)

IT'S YOUR CHOICE

Beloved, truth cannot be silenced for long. It is always revealed. Just look at the events surrounding Jesus' resurrection.

Though the local officials bought the soldiers' silence, word of his resurrection traveled fast, and people believed. *Jesus was alive!* Nothing could thwart the angel's good news!

More than two thousand years later, my Son is alive and well and ruling with me in heaven. But there are those on earth who still seek to shroud the facts in lies and silence. I am sending you out to end the silence and dispel the lies. I am sending you to reveal the truth of the Resurrection, because the truth will set people free.

Remember my heart—that none should perish—and pray for the lost among you, that one day their hearts and their minds will be open to me.

Read Matthew 28:1–15.

Open the heart of _____ to your love and your truth, O God.

JULY 14

Go and make disciples of all nations, baptizing them in the name of the Father and of the Son and of the Holy Spirit.
—**Matthew 28:19** (NIV)

MY GREAT COMMISSION

Sometimes my children wonder what I want them to do. My desire is that they tell others about my Son.

As Jesus was commissioning his followers in his day, he was also commissioning all who would follow days, years, and centuries later. Because his first listeners went out and made disciples, and those listeners went out and made disciples, eventually you heard the message. Now testify of what you have heard so that those who follow in your steps can also do the same.

Tell the people next door, in the next cubicle, or in the next county. Let them hear of Jesus' sacrifice for you, for them. Let them know that I care. And as you share the good news, be certain of this—I will go with you, even to the ends of the earth.

Read
Matthew
28:16–20.

Jesus, help me to tell others about you—my family, my friends, my neighbors.

JULY 15

The Spirit sent Jesus into the desert. He was in the desert forty days and was tempted by Satan. —**Mark 1:12–13** (NCV)

VICTORY

Child, I understand what you're going through when you're tempted. Like you, my Son faced a barrage of temptations—food, power, possessions. Yet even when he was weak from hunger, he endured in obedience to my will.

I am with you whenever temptation strikes. Though it is not a sin to be tempted, your challenge will be to stand against temptation. The wise response is to follow Jesus' example and use Scripture to defeat the enemy. Just call out to me. I will remind you of my truths and promises, and they will enable you to overcome any allure.

Come to me when you are tempted. Seek shelter in my Word, and I will give you the victory.

Read
Mark 1:1–13.

Lord, help me overcome this temptation that threatens to overpower me.

JULY 16

People were not made for the good of the Sabbath. The Sabbath was made for the good of people.
—**Mark 2:27** (CEV)

TRUE REST

My child, when I created the world, I created a cycle of work and rest. The Sabbath was created, not because I need to rest, but because I knew my people would need it.

The Pharisees accused my Son of breaking the Sabbath by healing the sick. How little did they know my heart! By providing healing, he was providing true rest for those who were burdened.

The Sabbath gives you a break from life's urgencies; it signals my yearning for you to forget—for a day—about those relentless to-do lists. I have ordained this day as a day of rest because I love you and want to spend time with you. If you let me, I will refresh you and energize you for the week ahead.

This is not just my day. It is *our* day. Let's spend it together.

Read
Mark 2:23 – 3:6.

Thank you for setting aside your day—our day—for rest and renewal.

The seed that fell on good soil
represents those who hear and
accept God's word.

—**Mark 4:20** (NLT)

GOOD SOIL

C hild, I am the Gardener of your heart. I care about the kind of soil that surrounds you and the fruit you bear. And I know what it takes to make you healthy.

Roots that run deep come from good soil—a heart that embraces my truth and my Word. The fruit of the Spirit—a life full of gracious, loving words and actions—is borne out of good soil as well. But you must beware of the pollutants that threaten your growth—pollutants like worry, impatience, and greed.

Trust me with the fallow ground of your heart. Let me pluck the weeds that threaten to choke your faith. As you trust me, I will sow good things into your life: faith, peace, generosity, perseverance. And through the life-giving light of my presence, I will keep you growing strong.

Read
Mark 4:1–25.

Help me examine the
soil of my heart. I want
to be open to your Word
in all areas of my life.

JULY 18

He is just the carpenter, the son of Mary and the brother of James, Joseph, Judas, and Simon. —**Mark 6:3** (NCV)

MORE THAN A CARPENTER

My dear child, I've seen the way people treat you sometimes. How their false notions and remarks have hurt you. How they've tried to put you in a box and bring you down.

Humans like to diminish each other with the use of one word: *just.* "She's just a woman." "He's just a child." "You're just a laborer" . . . Many labeled my Son as just a carpenter. He couldn't be the promised Messiah, they reasoned; messiahs don't come from small towns and do the kind of humble work that Jesus did. So they dismissed both him and his message.

But Jesus wasn't discouraged or deterred by their insults—and I don't want you to be either. Look to me and my estimation of you. Remember who you are in my eyes. You are my precious child.

Read
Mark 6:1–13.

Lord, when I think I'm of no value, remind me of your opinion of me.

JULY 19

*[King Herod] was greatly
distressed, but because of his
oaths and his dinner guests,
he did not want to refuse her.*
—**Mark 6:26** (NIV)

THE POWER OF WORDS

Beloved, words are very powerful. I used them to
create a universe; I use them to guide and console
my people. I use them to lift you up and keep you strong.

Words can help and heal or wound and destroy. King
Herod used his recklessly, wanting to show off in front
of his guests. And his rash and prideful promise cost my
servant John his life.

Though your circumstances today are different from
Herod's, take time and consider how you've wielded your
words lately. Have they been a sword or a soothing balm?
Have they built others up or torn others down?

I've entrusted you with the power of words, and I ask
you to use it carefully, my child. Words spoken in love,
expressions of comfort or encouragement or praise—these
can make all the difference in someone's life. Speak
wisely.

**Read
Mark 6:14–29.**

*Lord, guard my speech.
Cause me to consider
my words before I
speak them.*

*These people show honor to me
with words, but their hearts are
far from me.* —**Mark 7:6** (NCV)

I WANT YOUR HEART

Beloved, nothing is hidden from me. Not the desires of every heart. Not those who pay me only lip service. And certainly not those who truly seek a relationship with me.

From all appearances, the religious leaders of Jesus' day were the epitome of obedience. They used pious words, prayed long prayers, went through all the motions . . . But there was one thing they lacked—hearts that belonged to me.

Beloved, I want your heart. Plain and simple. When I am your passion—when you long to know and honor me above all else—you don't have to worry about piety and sacred gestures and how many acts of service you've performed. Your entire life becomes a song of praise to me! And out of that song will flow generosity and kindness and a love for others that does not end.

Seek me with all your heart.

Read
Mark 7:1–23.

*Lord, I give you my
heart.*

JULY 21

*[Jesus] asked them, "But who do
you say I am?" Peter replied,
"You are the Messiah."*

—**Mark 8:29** (NIV)

THE RESPONSE OF FAITH

Peter had the right answer. Even though he didn't fully understand what it meant for my Son to be the Messiah, he still recognized Jesus for who he was.

My Son asks the same question of every person in every generation that he asked of Peter: Who do you say that I am? Some believe Jesus was a wise teacher, a good man, or even a great prophet—worth listening to perhaps, but not my holy Son. Still others believe his resurrection was a hoax and call his followers fools.

Peter did not understand everything, but he got this much right: he knew that Jesus was who he claimed to be. Though you don't understand everything, my child, your response of faith is the foundation from which I build.

As you seek more of me, I will reveal more of myself to you. Believe it!

Read
Mark 8:22—9:1.

*Lord, I believe in your
Son's sacrifice for me.*

JULY 22

You must accept the kingdom of God as if you were a little child, or you will never enter it.
—**Mark 10:15** (NCV)

TRUST MY HEART

Jesus paved the way for you to become my child. So you can trust me like children naturally trust their parents.

Look to me to provide what you need: food, shelter, clothing, and protection. You don't have to understand every detail of your life or every facet of my character. Just trust my heart—and leave the details to me.

I am your loving Father, after all. The same one who sent my only Son to cover your sin and provide you with a home in heaven forever. If you can trust me with your eternal life, you can trust me with this present life. I am faithful, dependable, true.

Will you trust me?

Read
Mark 10:1–16.

Father God, help me to trust your heart when I don't understand.

JULY 23

Go, sell all you have and give to the poor, and you will have treasure in heaven. Then come, follow Me. —**Mark 10:21** (HCSB)

COME, FOLLOW ME

Dear one, I offer you life—life that does not require a certain status or wealth. In fact, I welcome the poor in spirit to feast at my table. Yet time and again, seekers turn down my offer, just as the rich young man did.

If only he had understood: I am not against you having possessions; it is a heart tied to possessions—or anything other than me—that grieves me. Once my gifts to you start competing with your devotion to me, they become distractions. And I never want you to be distracted.

Dear one, cling to me and the life I offer. Focus on me, rather than on what you think your possessions can provide. When you follow me with all your heart, you will always have everything you need.

Read
Mark 10:17–31.

Open my eyes to the distractions that prevent me from following you.

The Son of Man did not come to be served, but to serve, and to give his life as a ransom for many. —**Mark 10:45** (NIV)

THE HEART OF A SERVANT

As you get closer to me, you'll discover that my intent is not to lord myself over you. Anyone in authority can force a person to submit. My goal, however, is to win your heart through love. So I sent my Son.

He came, not to be served but to serve. Rather than asking people to cater to his every whim, he healed, blessed, and restored broken lives. And ultimately, he laid down his life. He was the suffering Servant predicted by the prophet Isaiah, willfully dying on the cross to free you from your sin.

I want you to know this love that gives itself away. When you do, it will be reflected in your life as well.

Read Mark 10:35–52.

Father, reveal to me your love, which gives itself away.

JULY 25

*You can pray for anything,
and if you believe that you've
received it, it will be yours.*
—**Mark 11:24** (NLT)

FAITH TO MOVE MOUNTAINS

Child, picture the biggest mountain you've ever seen.
Now picture it flying into the sea. I can literally do
that if I choose.

Now picture the problems in your life that appear as
big as mountains—the ones that seem just as immovable. I
can move those too, child.

Come to me with your burdens, even if you don't
understand how I can help. I don't require perfect faith;
faith the size of a tiny mustard seed is enough. Just call on
me with whatever faith you can muster, and know I will
respond with all that I am.

Have faith not only in my power, dear one, but in my
character. As your trust grows, you'll discover that my
goal is to move mountains and bring about good in your
life.

No Everest is too big for me.

Read
Mark 11:20–33.

*Almighty God, I place
my trust in your power
and your character.*

JULY 26

You must love him with all your heart, soul, mind, and strength.... Love others as much as you love yourself.
—**Mark 12:30–31** (CEV)

THE GREATEST GIFT

Beloved, when I tell you to love with all your heart, soul, mind, and strength, consider it an invitation. An invitation to drink from the bottomless well of my love. Let me fill you so that you can, in turn, love me with every part of your being.

Once you have that kind of love—my love—inside, it can't help but splash over the edges of your life onto everyone around you. And you learn to see your value in my eyes as well.

Love me. Love others. Discover how overwhelmingly you are loved. There is no greater gift, my child.

Read
Mark 12:28–37.

Father, fill me with your love so that it overflows to others.

Please take this cup of suffering away from me. Yet I want your will to be done, not mine.

—**Mark 14:36** (NLT)

ENTRUST YOURSELF TO ME

It's never easy for me to watch my children suffer. Even my Son asked to avoid the agony of the cross. Yet he laid down his will and his life, knowing that the path of least resistance would not reconcile the world to me. And in his surrender, he was resurrected into new life.

Sometimes you will struggle between your will and mine. I am with you in the struggle, child, just as I was with Jesus on that night before his crucifixion. And I love you with an undying love.

Trusting my will may involve suffering sometimes. Yet I promise you this: my will is the passage to true life. You can entrust yourself to me.

Read
Mark 14:27–42.

I trust your heart.
Lord, not my will but
yours be done.

JULY 28

Pilate asked them again, "Then what do you want me to do with the One you call the King of the Jews?" —**Mark 15:12** (HCSB)

MY GIFT TO YOU

I am the God of love. A generous, benevolent God. It is my nature to give often and to give much—to the believing and unbelieving alike. But sadly, not everyone is willing to receive.

Jesus was my ultimate gift to the world. Many people welcomed him as a conquering king—at first. But once he failed to fit the mold, they just as quickly turned away. This suffering, humiliated man was still the gift—the one, true King—but they just wouldn't see it.

Pilate's question stands before you today: *What will you do with Jesus?* Will you accept him as my gift? Or will you turn away because he's not exactly what you expected?

Your answer makes all the difference, dear one. Enjoy my Gift, now and forever!

R e a d
M a r k 1 5 : 6 – 2 4 .

I accept the gift of your Son. Thank you for sending him to save me.

JULY 29

"How can I know this?" Zecha-
riah asked the angel. "For I am
an old man, and my wife is well
along in years."

—**Luke 1:18** (HCSB)

WHEN YOU DON'T UNDERSTAND

Nothing is beyond my ability, child. I have no limitations. I always say what I mean, and every word from my mouth comes true.

Zechariah lost sight of these truths, even after I'd sent the angel to assure him of my plan. And his reaction grieved me. In human terms, he and his wife may have been too old to have a child, but I am not bound by earthly constraints. Neither age, nor inabilities, nor circumstances can prevent my word from being fulfilled; I can do all things.

My plans may not always align with your reasoning; sometimes they will seem downright illogical. But instead of worrying about how, when, or why I will fulfill them, let your lack of understanding drive you into the safety of my arms. True spiritual maturity means trusting me in every area of your life. Especially when you don't understand.

Read
Luke 1:5-25.

I trust you, God—
whether or not I
understand your ways.

JULY 30

Mary responded, "I am the Lord's servant. May everything you have said about me come true." —Luke 1:38 (NLT)

IN MY HANDS

Precious one, do you know who is responsible for your life? Sometimes you live as if it's you and you alone—a surefire path to exhaustion, isolation, and bitterness. But I say to you, child: you belong to me, and you are *my* responsibility. So trust in my goodness. I will only work good in your life. Trust also in my greatness, because I can do anything. Orchestrating the details of your life is no more difficult than setting the planets in their orbits—and I did that with ease.

Follow the example of my servant Mary, who willingly entrusted herself to me in a time when she least understood my plans. Have faith in me and me alone. And remember: when you feel stressed, nothing thrills me more than hearing you say, "Lord, I am your servant. I place myself—and my life—in your hands."

Read
Luke 1:26-45.

Lord, I am your servant. I place myself in your hands.

JULY 31

*Blessed is the Lord God of Israel,
for He has visited and redeemed
His people.* —**Luke 1:68** (NKJV)

MY PROMISES ARE SURE

Nothing can stop my plans, loved one. I planned
for my promised Son—the Messiah, the Light of
heaven—to come to earth and guide the lost into the way
of peace. And I planned for him to have a herald who
would declare his arrival to my people.

I gave Zechariah these prophetic words, along with
my promise that his son would prepare the way for mine.
Zechariah spoke as though it had already happened,
knowing my promises are sure. And soon enough, both
Jesus and Zechariah's son John would fulfill their callings
exactly as I said.

If you ever start to wonder where to turn or who to
trust, beloved, think of me. Then turn to my Word. Every
promise I have ever made will come true.

Read
Luke 1:57–80.

*God, thank you that
I can trust all your
promises to come true.*

AUGUST

AUGUST 1

The shepherds returned, glorifying and praising God for all they had seen and heard, just as they had been told.

—**Luke 2:20** (HCSB)

THE BEST NEWS EVER

By announcing my Son's birth to the shepherds, I made a statement to the world: I share good news with all people—even those with little status in society. I could have sent the angelic choir to the leaders in Jerusalem, but I chose instead to declare my message to some receptive hearts tending sheep outside of Bethlehem. Those shepherds went to find my Son, they believed, and they passed the news on to others—news that amazed many.

My good news is for everyone in your world. Whether rich or poor, healthy or sick, powerful or downtrodden, I long for all to know me. Word of my Son's birth may amaze or confound them, but share the message, my child.

It is the best news they will ever hear.

Read
Luke 2:1–20.

Lord Jesus, help me share your good news with those around me.

AUGUST 2

[Anna] talked about the child to everyone who had been waiting expectantly for God to rescue Jerusalem. —**Luke 2:38** (NLT)

TALK ABOUT ME

I love the joy my people experience when they see my promises fulfilled. For many, many years, Anna waited expectantly for the coming of my Son, fully believing that I would deliver the promised Messiah to my people. I watched with delight as she bore witness with Simeon to the tiny life Mary held in her arms.

Like Anna, you can tell people about my grace. Let people know that I love them and came to rescue them from their sin and shame. Remind them that I delight in those who wait expectantly for me to respond, and that often, in the waiting, I do wonderful things.

Imagine the lives we can touch together, dear one. You do the talking, and I will do the saving.

Read
Luke 2:21–38.

Lord, give me the words that will draw people to you.

Why were you looking for me?
Did you not know that I must be
in my Father's house?
—**Luke 2:49** (ESV)

I AM HERE

Child, I am at work in your life, especially in the times when you don't sense my presence or understand my path. I am here in your questions. Even when you are anxiously seeking me like Joseph and Mary sought Jesus—wondering where I have gone—I am with you. Do not fear.

Sometimes you fret, wondering if I'm still watching over you. Things happen that don't make sense, causing you concern, fear, panic. My child, I am never apart from you; I never lose control or forget you. You are engraved on the palms of my hands. You are the apple of my eye.

No need to come looking. Sit quietly before me. I'm here.

Read
Luke 2:41–52.

Help me relax and
trust that you're at
work—even when I
can't see you.

AUGUST 4

*On the Sabbath day he went to
the synagogue, as he always did.*
—Luke 4:16 (NCV)

A SPECIAL DAY

I made the Sabbath a special day. As my Son would
later say, I did not make you for the Sabbath; I made
the Sabbath for you.

I know how busy you are, how many responsibilities
you have, how many people depend on you. I also know,
my precious creation, that you cannot keep up the pace
without some rest. So I gave you a whole day just for
letting down your load and being with me.

As a part of that special day, refresh yourself by
focusing on me. You can find Sabbath rest in church, as
my Son did in the synagogue. Worshiping me will not
only remind you of my love and rejuvenate your spirit but
give you rest, my child.

Follow my Son's example.

Read
Luke 4:14–30.

*Father, I will be at
church on Sunday—
worshiping and resting
in you.*

AUGUST 5

Everyone was gripped with great wonder and awe, and they praised God, exclaiming, "We have seen amazing things today!" —**Luke 5:26** (NLT)

AMAZING THINGS

Walk with me today, my child, and see what I can do. The healing of the paralyzed man was just a glimpse of the amazing things I am capable of. My Son would bring about the greatest healing of all—healing from the power of sin for everyone who believes. It is a miracle that I do every day, even to this day.

People don't always recognize my miracles, to be sure, but anytime I move in your life, it is an event to be celebrated. From the daily blessings I give you, to the calamities that don't happen because of my intervention, to the surprises that sometimes get chalked up to coincidence, I am powerfully at work on your behalf—reaching out to you with a love that never ends.

Though others may overlook my grace, you know me, child. You see my hand everywhere. Let me show you the amazing things I will do today.

Read
Luke 5:17–26.

Lord, I have seen the remarkable things you have done.

AUGUST 6

I have come to call not those who think they are righteous, but those who know they are sinners and need to repent.

—**Luke 5:32** (NLT)

THE WORTH OF WORDS

I am a God of my word. I keep my promises. The rainbow proves it.

The great flood was the first and the last to destroy the earth. I will never again send a catastrophic, earth-drenching flood. You have my solemn oath on that.

In a day when people tend to say what they will to get ahead, to get by, or to get off, you can always count on my words. Vows and promises mean much to me. You will notice as you read my Book how often I speak of words. I take what you say quite seriously.

As I have kept my promises, keep yours. Be a person of your word. Like Father, like child.

Read
Luke 5:27–32.

Father, I choose to follow you—today and for the rest of my life.

I tell you, I have not found
such great faith even in Israel.
—**Luke 7:9** (NIV)

FAITH THAT DELIGHTS ME

L et me tell you about the kind of faith that delights me, child. It's the kind of faith that persists in believing in me when all hope is lost. The kind that comes from a heart that has relinquished all other avenues save one—me. The kind that doesn't need to peek around doorways or insist on "just a glimpse" to satisfy curiosity and bolster belief.

The Roman soldier's faith delighted me because it came with an appreciation of my Son. The toughened centurion believed that Jesus had the power and the authority to do what was asked—and Jesus gladly responded.

Faith that always delights me, child, is faith that trusts the light even in the darkness. Dare to trust me, and experience my great delight.

Read
Luke 7:1–17.

Father, help me
remember your
strength and presence
so that my faith can
soar.

AUGUST 8

Her many sins are forgiven,
so she showed great love. But
the person who is forgiven only
a little will love only a little.
—**Luke 7:47** (NCV)

YOUR OFFERING

Your grateful heart is precious to me. The struggles you have overcome have strengthened you, your character, and your relationships with others—including me. The way you have studied my Word, poured yourself out for others, and kept your heart vulnerable before me demonstrates your love for me.

Now let's build on that foundation, beloved. Will you offer me your "alabaster jar"—the thing that you're most reluctant to give up: your will, that dream or goal, that unforgiveness, that valued possession? In return, I will offer you the riches of my peace, my power, and my presence. Won't you accept?

Read
Luke 7:36–50.

Lord, I hold some
things too tightly.
They're yours.

AUGUST 9

The disciples went and woke him, saying, "Master, Master, we're going to drown!"

—**Luke 8:24** (NIV)

YOUR LIFELINE

I am here to rescue you, beloved. You may feel like the disciples in the midst of the storm, fearing that their boat would be swamped. The rain is thrashing, the water is rising, and your options are running out. Or, like the demon-possessed man, you may feel misunderstood, rejected by society, and hopeless to change. Whatever your circumstances, you're resigned that you can't endure in your own power—you cannot save yourself.

Your situation may be dire, loved one, but let me remind you: you have nothing to fear. I have power over every obstacle, every storm, every evil influence. You don't have to change on your own. I can change you. Call on me, and I will rescue you. I am your lifeline.

Read
Luke 8:22–39.

Master, Master, I feel like I'm drowning. I believe you can save me.

AUGUST 10

Don't be afraid; just believe.
—**Luke 8:50** (NIV)

IN YOUR DEEPEST SORROW

I feel your grief and sadness, my beloved. I see your brokenness and confusion as you whisper *Where are you?* and *Why?*

Where am I? I'm here, right in the midst of your pain. Though your sense of loss seems as overwhelming as a tsunami, know that I am constant—and constantly paying attention.

Why do I allow this? My beloved, sorrow is the product of a broken world—and an enemy who seeks to destroy your soul. Though for now illness exists and death is certain, darkness does not have the final say. So I ask you to walk with me. Let my light and my love wash over you, bringing you healing one day at a time.

Read
Luke 8:40–56.

Lord, give me what I need to get through today. Please lighten my burden.

AUGUST 11

Awe gripped the people as they saw this majestic display of God's power. —**Luke 9:43** (NLT)

MAJESTY REVEALED

How I treasure the precious times we spend together, child! I delight to give you glimpses of my majesty: in the intricate design of a spider's web, in the patient smile of a grandparent, in the crash and swell of the ocean waves.

If you take time to look, you'll see how constantly I reveal myself to you. Not just in your greatest joys, but in your sorrows and deepest need. I can supply you with exactly what you need, exactly when you need it—sometimes in the most unexpected way.

Those times when I reveal my majesty are not coincidences. When you acknowledge me and my glory, you reflect me to a watching world. And others will want what you have—a relationship with me, the living God.

Read
Luke 9:28–45.

Lord of mercy and grace, Creator of all things majestic, thank you for the ways you reveal yourself.

AUGUST 12

Do not rejoice that the spirits submit to you, but rejoice that your names are written in heaven. —**Luke 10:20** (NIV)

A GREATER CAUSE TO CELEBRATE

Dear child, I love that you enjoy doing good works in my name. Your desire to please me and your tenderness for others demonstrates the difference that citizenship in my kingdom makes.

When you rejoice in my power working through you, I rejoice. But the fact that you will be with me for eternity is cause for a greater celebration. The day you accepted my love and grace caused me to sing songs of joy—songs that still continue. I have written your name in heaven. You will always be mine.

Now *that* is something to celebrate!

Read
Luke 10:1–24.

Lord, thank you for writing my name in heaven.

AUGUST 13

Which of these three do you think was a neighbor to the man who fell into the hands of robbers?
—**Luke 10:36–37** (NIV)

ACROSS THE DIVIDE

Because I love, I desire that my people love. That's why the divisions that separate people grieve me so deeply. I sent my Son to scale those walls; I enlist my children to join him in knocking them down; and I gave my Spirit to make sure they are never rebuilt.

My love is not a fortress designed to keep people out, but a hedge of protection around those who trust me. It invites you to take risks, to reach across the divide and embrace even those you fear or don't understand.

Your neighbors need mercy. My mercy. Just as the Good Samaritan stopped to help an enemy in need, I'm asking you to show the same kind of love. Rest assured, I will be right beside you. Together we'll replace those walls of misunderstanding, prejudice, and fear with a hedge of grace and love.

Read
Luke 10:25–37.

Lord, help me to reach out in love to my neighbors.

AUGUST 14

Jesus said, "This is how you should pray." —**Luke 11:2** (NLT)

TALK TO ME

There is no big mystery to prayer, beloved. It's a matter of talking, and then listening; telling me what you're thinking, and then seeking my thoughts; sharing what you need, and then asking me what's best for you.

Prayer is the language of our relationship. The better you know me, the easier our conversation flows. You'll discover my character described vividly throughout the Scriptures, so look for me there. I am your loving Father who has strong shoulders you can lean on. I am your forgiving Father who wants to help you do better. I am your understanding Father who builds your character. I am your just Father who will deal with the wrongs of the world.

Just talk to me. I'm listening.

Read
Luke 11:1–13.

Father in heaven, holy is your name. May your will be done.

AUGUST 15

Blessed are those who hear the word of God and keep it!
—**Luke 11:28** (NKJV)

OBEDIENCE BRINGS BLESSING

Obedience brings rich blessing, my child. Sometimes doing what I ask is easy. Your desire for a happy family leads you to gladly serve your spouse or parents with humility. Your tender heart for the homeless inspires you to give graciously of your time and treasure. Sometimes, though, following through is not so second-nature. Still, you can be sure of this: when you hear my Word and it pierces to the joints and marrow of your soul—when it inspires you to act in ways that honor me—I will bless you.

The treasure trove of my Word is where you find my wisdom. It's where I supply you with strength for your day. So open it every day. It never becomes old or stale, and never loses its power.

Because my Word is full of power, it will give you power to hear it and to keep it. And in keeping it, you will be blessed.

Read
Luke 11:14–32.

Lord, thank you for your Word, which shows me how to live for you.

AUGUST 16

This very night your life will be demanded from you. Then who will get what you have prepared for yourself?

—**Luke 12:20** (NIV)

WHAT ARE YOUR PLANS?

I can see it all, my child—all the days of your life, all the intentions and expectations you have—like fence posts stretching mile after mile. Your calendar is filled with plans for yourself, your family and friends. You even schedule time with me.

You are well prepared to handle this life—and I am pleased. But what about the next life? What activities on your calendar have eternal value? You know the ones I mean: Are you building the faith of younger believers? Encouraging those who are far away from me? Storing up Scripture in your heart?

Beloved, I am never threatened by your plans. But I want to help you make the kind of plans that will benefit you in this life and into eternity. Bring me your plans, and I will share mine with you.

Read
Luke 12:1–21.

Father, help me sort out what's important for today. Your will, not mine.

*Can all your worries add a
single moment to your life?*
—**Luke 12:25** (NLT)

WARRIOR OVER YOUR WORRIES

Beloved, I orchestrated the universe. I set the sun and
moon in place and ordered the sunrise and sunset.
Day by day I balance the delicate nuances of nature so
that each plant and animal, from the smallest to the
largest, has its unique needs met. My plan allows for each
of them to flourish.

My desire is for you to do the same—to flourish.
This can't happen when you fall into a cycle of worry.
When you expend all your energy fretting about things
you can't control, you have nothing left for the things you
can control.

I'm asking you to trust me to provide what you
need when you need it. Let me be Lord of your life and
Warrior over your worries.

Read
Luke 12:22–34.

*Father, help me see
that when I worry, I'm
actually doubting you.*

AUGUST 18

[The kingdom of God] is like a tiny mustard seed that a man planted in a garden; it grows and becomes a tree.

—**Luke 13:19** (NLT)

SMALL BEGINNINGS

My kingdom began simply, with a tiny baby in a cow's stall in an obscure town in Judea.

My Son walked the dusty roads of the land, called followers to himself, taught the truth, died, then rose again and ascended to me.

Those followers soon traveled to far-away countries and heralded the good news my Son brought to all people. And on it goes even today.

Like a tiny mustard seed that grows into a plant big enough for birds to nest in, so my kingdom started small but now extends to the far corners of the earth. One day, every knee will bow and every tongue confess that my kingdom has come.

You are a citizen of that great kingdom, child. Invite everyone you know to join you—and rejoice!

Read
Luke 13:1–21.

Holy One, I look forward to being with you in your kingdom.

AUGUST 19

*How often I have longed to gather
your children together, as a hen
gathers her chicks under her
wings, but you were not willing.*
—**Luke 13:34** (NIV)

OUR TIME TOGETHER

My dearest child, sit and close your eyes for a
minute. Recall a moment when you felt sweet
peace and unadulterated joy. It warms your heart and
makes you smile; it is a moment you wish would last
forever.

That's exactly what I want with you: times spent
that will last forever. If you let me, I can bring you joy
and peace in ways that you may not expect—through
the encouragement of a stranger or the kiss of a child;
through the forgiveness of a friend or release from your
fear; whether darkness is overhead or the sun is shining
bright.

I long to spend time with you, now and forever, but I
will not push you, child. My heart reaches out, yearning
for you to receive my love.

Eternity begins now, beloved. Won't you embrace it?

Read
Luke 13:22–35.

*Father, I receive your
love, and am grateful
that our time together
will last forever.*

AUGUST 20

All who make themselves great will be made humble, but those who make themselves humble will be made great.

—**Luke 14:11** (NCV)

THE DESIRES OF YOUR HEART

In a world where people jockey for position and power, I call you to be different, my beloved. Look at your hands. Belonging to me means they bear the calluses of a carpenter and the imprint of cruel, heavy nails.

There are times when you strive so hard to exalt yourself, to claim a place and make a name for yourself. Yet that path holds nothing but struggle; maintaining a position is tenuous at best.

I want to relieve you of that burden, child. Come to me; ask me what my plans are for you. Humble yourself, and I will give you the desires of your heart.

In your humility you will find rest.

Read
Luke 14:1–14.

Lord, I humble myself before you. Show me your plan for my life.

AUGUST 21

If you do not carry your own cross and follow me, you cannot be my disciple.

—**Luke 14:27** (NLT)

BE MY DISCIPLE

When I called you to myself, it was out of my great love for you. And though I want to fulfill all your dreams and give you the desires of your heart, I never promised my followers a problem-free life. In fact, I know you will have trials and tribulations. But here is one thing I do promise: I will never leave you nor forsake you in the midst of those troubles.

It's not easy to follow me, I know. I will require you to count the cost. Will you put your faith in me anyway? Will you give me your all? When hard times come, will you let me walk every step of the way with you?

Come, my beloved child, and be my disciple. For when you do, you will see my blessings poured out in abundance. Unspeakable blessings that I have reserved just for you.

Read
Luke 14:15–33.

Lord, I've counted the cost and have chosen to follow you.

AUGUST 22

*There is joy in the presence
of the angels of God over one
sinner who repents.*

—**Luke 15:10** (NKJV)

GREAT REJOICING

Join with me for a moment, my child, to envision the
gladness in heaven when a sinner repents. Listen to
the commanding sounds of the trumpets, the brass and
strings and woodwinds in their unending harmony. Picture
my angels singing and dancing in glorious light, the
heavenly chorus celebrating with one accord—all because a
lost lamb has come home.

Child, heaven rejoiced the day you turned to me
through the sacrifice of my Son. Heaven rejoices as you
overcome each temptation, as you grow in faith, as you
tell others about the One who saved you from sin.

Listen, child. All of heaven is singing over you.

Read
Luke 15:1–10.

*Lord, may I bring you
and all of heaven joy
and gladness today.*

While he was still a long way off, his father saw him coming.
—**Luke 15:20** (NLT)

I WON'T GIVE UP ON YOU

Oh my precious child, when you're apart from me, I yearn for your return. When you hurry off, determined to walk alone, it saddens me to see you go.

Yet I haven't given up on you. No good parent ever does. I watch for you day in and day out, because you are my child and I love you dearly. Months may pass; years may come and go, but you can always come back to me, no matter where you've been or what you've done.

On the day that I see you approaching in the distance, I, your heavenly Father, will run to meet you, to embrace you, and to celebrate your return with open arms. I never give up on you.

Read
Luke 15:11–32.

Lord, thank you for refusing to give up on me.

Whoever is faithful in a very little is faithful also in much; and whoever is dishonest in a very little is dishonest also in much. —**Luke 16:10** (NRSV)

SHOW YOUR INTEGRITY

Adored child, everything in the universe is mine. Giving good things to my children is my great pleasure. However, sometimes I will test you with these gifts to see how you handle yourself. I do this to help you grow.

Remember how, when you were growing up, the adults in your life gave you more and more responsibility as you proved yourself trustworthy? Your progress toward dependability was marked with delight. I, too, am always ready to celebrate these milestones of maturity.

I have much for you to do, dear one. I am willing to trust you with it because you have shown yourself faithful.

Read
Luke 16:1–13.

I want to be a person of integrity, dear Lord, in both small and large matters.

If they won't listen to Moses and the prophets, they won't listen even if someone rises from the dead. —**Luke 16:31** (NLT)

THE GREATEST MIRACLE

Many cry out to me, "If you are God, give me a miracle and then I'll believe! Prove yourself to me; then you can have my trust!" But what these people don't understand is that my miracles are signposts marking the way to my kingdom for those who long to believe; they won't soften a heart that is hardened against me.

In your heart, child, you search for more than just a miracle—you search for *me*. And I am happy to respond, for I am everything you seek. I fill the emptiness within you with my love. I supply your yearning for answers with my Word. I overflow your doubts with my peace and your desperation with my joy. And through it all, you receive the greatest of miracles—the miracle of grace.

Read
Luke 16:19–31.

God, your grace is the greatest miracle I could ever receive.

AUGUST 26

Didn't I heal ten men? Where are the other nine? Has no one returned to give glory to God except this foreigner?

—**Luke 17:17** (NLT)

THE BEAUTY OF GRATITUDE

A smile of gratitude. A heart filled with quiet praise. Words of thanks spoken aloud. These are all beautiful to me.

Not everyone remembers me as they enjoy my gifts—in fact, real gratitude is rare, as the ten healed men proved. But I bless those who do thank me—and I am blessed when *you* do.

Gratitude has a beauty that far surpasses the painted sky at sunset or the moon's silver gleam on the ocean. It has its roots deep in faith and is the expression of a heart connected to mine. That's what I see in you, child. When you recognize and thank me in the blessings of your life, you are beautiful. And I am blessed.

Read
Luke 17:1–19.

Lord, you are the source of everything; thank you for all you've given me.

AUGUST 27

It will be "business as usual"
right up to the day when the
Son of Man is revealed.

—**Luke 17:30** (NLT)

ARE YOU READY?

Beloved, I sent my Son so that your life would
be more than "business as usual." The struggle
to survive was meant to lead you to the cross and a
relationship with him. It was meant to create in you a
longing for his return.

I also gave you my Word to help you live out your
life in preparation for that great day. Come, my beloved,
and renew your mind daily, readying yourself for Jesus'
return. Help others, meet together in fellowship, share out
of your abundance—model your life after my words.

My Son will return as sure as the dawn. Live as if
today will be that day.

Read
Luke 17:20–37.

Lord, I'll live my life
for you as I expectantly
wait for your return.

Will not God bring about justice for his chosen ones, who cry out to him day and night?

—**Luke 18:7** (NIV)

ON TIME

My child, I still act in an unjust world. The evil that surrounds my people does not mean that I have turned a blind eye or that I no longer care. I am always aware of the hurting and the lost—and I hear their cries for mercy.

Remember this whenever you fear that I have not heard you or—worse—that I am deliberately ignoring you. My love is constant, never-changing. I hear your every prayer, and I answer in my way and time.

When my timing does not match your expectations, don't give up on prayer, beloved, and don't give up on me. I always arrive on time.

Read
Luke 18:1–14.

Father, in all things, I will send up my prayers to you.

The Son of Man has come to seek and to save that which was lost. —**Luke 19:10** (NLT)

SEEKING YOU

A true shepherd can't rest if one of his sheep is lost. He will do everything he can—even endure the dark of night and dangerous predators—to find that lamb and bring it home safely.

As the Good Shepherd, I have gone the extra mile for you. Before you sought me, I was seeking you. Before you knew you were lost, I was saving you. When you realized your hopelessness, I heard your prayer. And, without hesitation, I came to you, lovingly placed you on my shoulders, and brought you into the fold.

I still seek even those I have "found." I seek time with you; I seek your growth and your protection; I seek your heart. I am the Shepherd of your soul.

Read
Luke 19:1–10.

Lord, by your grace I am found. Thank you for protecting me.

AUGUST 30

Some of the scribes answered, "Teacher, You have spoken well." —**Luke 20:39** (HCSB)

WHAT'S YOUR QUESTION?

My beloved child, I am not like those leaders who challenged my Son, hoping to disprove him and exalt themselves. The proud love to prey on those they consider weak, but I never look to trap the unwary or embarrass those who thirst for knowledge. So don't be afraid to ask me any question you have. And don't think that I will be offended by your asking. I can handle your toughest dilemmas and even your deepest doubts.

When you come to me with the difficult questions, you only get to know me better. And the more you come to know me, the more you'll see that what I cherish is your genuine pursuit of me.

Read
Luke 20:20–40.

My God, it is my desire to open myself up and know you more.

I will give you the wisdom to say things that none of your enemies will be able to stand against or prove wrong.

—**Luke 21:15** (NCV)

NOW AND FOREVER

When you follow me, dear child, you will suffer some form of persecution. Some people may laugh at you or talk behind your back; some may even be so bold as to call you foolish.

My precious Son was treated with disdain—even to the point of death. When you face persecution because of your faith in me, know that I will enable you to stand before your enemies without fear. I will give you the wisdom to say what needs to be said, with words so true and clear that your persecutors will be unable to prove them wrong. I will strengthen you and comfort you and give you peace, but most importantly, I will be with you.

Now and forever.

Read
Luke 21:5–24.

Lord, thank you for providing everything I need the moment I need it.

SEPTEMBER

SEPTEMBER 1

They will see the Son of Man coming in a cloud with power and great glory.

—**Luke 21:27** (ESV)

LIFT YOUR EYES

Blessed child, from the beginning I have called you my own. And I have loved you more than you can know. My mercy has drawn you to me and my grace has guided your life. Continue to live a holy life—helping those in need, sharing out of your wealth, and loving others as I have loved you. You are my child, my family, my own.

Soon my Son will return and lead you to your heavenly home. So pray, child. Lift your eyes toward the heavens and your heart to me. Read my Word and keep it in your heart. Heaven and earth will pass away, but my words will never pass away.

With me, you have a wonderful eternity.

Read
Luke 21:25–38.

Lord, thank you that I can face the future with confidence.

[Judas] agreed and began looking for an opportunity to betray Jesus. —**Luke 22:6** (NLT)

YOUR HURTS ARE MINE

Child of mine, I have grieved over every betrayal you've suffered. When you were hurt, I hurt. When you cried, I cried. Your pain is my pain; your wounds are my wounds. I love you with an everlasting love. When someone doesn't treat you right, I rise up with indignation just as any father would.

I am well acquainted with rejection; I was with my Son in his darkest moments and felt the same sting of betrayal he did. But just as I was able to transform Judas's betrayal of Jesus into something good, I also have the power to transform your situation.

Give me your wounded heart, and I will give you my peace.

Read Luke 22:1–13.

Loving Father, vindicate me and heal my aching heart.

SEPTEMBER 3

Herod asked Jesus many questions, but Jesus said nothing.
—**Luke 23:9** (NCV)

LIGHT OF TRUTH

When others falsely accuse you, child, do not worry or fear their slander. Instead, hold your head high and be encouraged, knowing you are my special treasure. I am always with you and am committed to protect you. My keen eye is on every detail of your present circumstance.

Do not fret, believing that those who hurt you are getting away with it. They will not. At this very moment, I am working behind the scenes to shed my light of truth on your situation. And my truth will prevail. All I ask is that you patiently allow me to work things out in my time. In the meantime, let my grace be sufficient for you.

Read
Luke 23:1–12.

I trust you, Lord, to shine your light of truth.

BLESSED FORGIVENESS

My precious one, it is possible to forgive those who taunt and abuse you. It isn't always easy—indeed, it can be painful—but if you are willing, I will empower you to bear with grace the wounds you've suffered.

Forgiveness wasn't easy for my Son either. But it was necessary. My plan and purpose for him required that the cross come first.

In my purpose for you, I want you to have the freedom that forgiveness brings. Forgiveness allows you to let go and follow me, every step of the way. In the end, you will be able to pray with a sincere heart the very prayer that Jesus did that day on the cross: "Father, forgive them."

Read Luke 23:32–49.

Lord, hold me tightly as I learn to forgive the injustices done to me.

SEPTEMBER 5

Suddenly, their eyes were opened, and they recognized him. —**Luke 24:31** (NLT)

I AM WITH YOU

Beloved child, do you remember when you first accepted the love I offered through my Son? That was a special day for both of us—one I'd waited for since the day you were born. You see, I walked beside you, protected you, and attended to your needs all along. But oh, how thrilling it was when your eyes opened and you acknowledged that I am God—*your God!* That's when our relationship really grew. Now I look forward to our special times together more than ever.

I love to reveal myself to you through my Word—to help you know more about me. Though you can't physically see me, look with the eyes of your heart: I am as close as the mention of my name.

I love you with an everlasting love, my child. I always have and I always will.

Read
Luke 24:13 – 34.

Open your Word to me, Lord. I'm longing for a revelation of your hope, power, and presence.

SEPTEMBER 6

To all who believed him and accepted him, he gave the right to become children of God.
—John 1:12 (NLT)

MY CHILD

I call you my child because that is what you are. Your age doesn't matter. When you are nine and when you are ninety, you are always my "child." From the moment you believed in and accepted Jesus' sacrifice, you became my child—precious, loved, valued, cared for, watched over, guided; yes, even disciplined at times. My love is the love of a perfect Father. My love sent my Son to make this relationship between us possible. Light came into the darkness. Joy came to the world.

My child (and make no mistake, I love calling you that), take my hand and let's walk through the rest of this life together.

Read
John 1:1–18.

Father, today I place my hand in yours.

SEPTEMBER 7

*Behold! The Lamb of God who
takes away the sin of the world!*
—**John 1:29** (NKJV)

SPOTLESS

You're clean, my child. Spotless. Pure. I know some
days you wonder if it's true. Some days you face
that old nature that acts in ways you know are wrong.
Sometimes you battle the temptations of your old life. And
sometimes you fall and need me to pick you up, dust you
off, and help you back onto the path I've set for you.

But when I look at you, I see my Son's sacrifice that
has made you clean. You are spotless before me. That's
what I see, precious one.

Read
John 1:19 – 34.

*Thank you for sending
your Son so I can be
spotless before you.*

SEPTEMBER 8

The next day Jesus decided to go to Galilee. He found Philip and said to him, "Come, follow me."
—John 1:43 (NLT)

I FOUND YOU

My sheep know my voice, child. It is that quiet whisper inviting you to accept the truth and wisdom I offer. I speak through a song on the radio, through the words of a pastor, or through the sudden knowledge that all will be well, even when it looks as if nothing will ever be good again. Through my Spirit I invite, I bid, I welcome you to believe in my Son, just as I did Philip on that day in Galilee. But I do not force your decision.

Although I planned your days before you were born, I wait until you accept my invitation to draw near. I keep coaxing you, calling you, and assuring you of my love— encouraging you toward the light of my salvation.

Each faltering step you take toward me is cause for rejoicing. You can always find me, child, because I found you first.

Read
John 1:35–51.

Thank you, Lord, for inviting me to follow you.

SEPTEMBER 9

Jesus and his disciples had also been invited to the wedding.
—John 2:2 (NIV)

LET'S CELEBRATE!

I am the God who celebrates, my child. I built into the fabric of my law times of great rejoicing throughout the year—special feasts and festivals for my people. And I celebrate with you on your important occasions.

My Son and his followers were invited to a wedding in Cana. Such a wonderful event! And my Son made it even better by helping the host out of an embarrassing situation. Might seem minor to some, but Jesus knew that it mattered.

Invite me to all of your celebrations, dear one! Let me be a part of every joyous occasion in your life, filling your celebrations with the joy of my Spirit. When you invite my presence and seek my blessing, everything—just like with the water that became wine—is better.

Let's celebrate together.

Read
John 2:1–11.

Father God, you have a standing invitation to all of my celebrations.

God so loved the world, that he gave his only Son, that whoever believes in him should not perish but have eternal life.

—John 3:16 (ESV)

THAT'S HOW MUCH

My love for you is beyond your imagining. I gave my Son for you.

Ponder those words for a moment, my child. *My Son. Given. For you.* So you would not perish. So you could have eternal life with me.

That's how much I wanted you. Sin had separated us, but I made a way—the only way—with the gift of my only Son. It grieved me to let him die. It grieved me to turn my face from him as he took on all sin. But I did it for you. His life for your life.

By his pain you were rescued. By his sacrifice you were saved. By his wounds you were healed.

I gave my Son so that you would not perish but have eternal life. That's how much I cherish you.

Read John 3:1–21.

Lord, I live in awe of your sacrifice for me.

SEPTEMBER 11

He must increase, but I must decrease. —**John 3:30** (NASB)

OUR STORIES

My servant John understood the great honor he'd been given as the appointed forerunner of my Son. Not only did I call John to prepare people's hearts for Jesus' arrival, but John knew he would need to point his followers to my Son instead, for Jesus was the one who came to save.

Beloved, I have given you the honor of touching the lives of those around you, pointing them to my Son. You know what he has done in your life; it's a story of my grace and power that only you can tell. A story unlike anyone else's. Look for me to send certain people your way—souls I've hand-selected who need to hear what I have done specifically for you.

My story. Your story. Told together, we will welcome more people into my kingdom.

Read John 3:22–36.

Sovereign Lord, thank you for giving me a story.

SEPTEMBER 12

Those who drink the water I give will never be thirsty again.
—**John 4:14** (NLT)

DRINK DEEPLY

There is nothing quite like a cold cup of water on a hot summer day, is there, my child? That refreshing feeling—when your physical thirst is quenched so perfectly—is what I want to give you each day. My living water is like a fresh, bubbling spring of joy within.

So drink deeply of me. When you are weary from a hard day's work, drink deeply. When sadness overwhelms you, drink deeply. When anger threatens your peace, drink deeply. My resources are unlimited and my grace is sufficient. So draw from my well, and drink until your thirst is quenched. Allow me to flood your soul with rivers of living water. And soon, you—like the Samaritan woman—will be sharing your joy with everyone you know.

Read John 4:1–26.

O God, my soul is parched. Please quench my spiritual thirst with your living water.

The man took Jesus at his word and departed. —John 4:50 (NIV)

TAKE ME AT MY WORD

Beloved, I can and do set things in motion with just a word. At my word, the world was created. At my word, the sun halted in its tracks in the sky. At my word, my every purpose is accomplished. That's why I love for my words to be taken seriously.

That's what faith is, child—taking me at my word. And such faith always moves me to action. When the desperate father came to my Son longing for help, he believed what Jesus said—that his words had the power to heal. The man left expecting a miracle and was not disappointed.

You can trust what I say, my child. Come to me with that problem, that worry. Take me at my word. You won't be disappointed.

Read
John 4:43–54.

God, I believe you can do all that I ask of you.

Do you want to get well?
—John 5:6 (HCSB)

OPEN HEARTS

As my Son scanned the crowd at the Bethesda pool that day, he was not looking at people's frailties—he was looking at their hearts. He saw one man who was open to physical and spiritual healing, and my Son reached out with love.

I ask people around the world every day—through my Word, through the situations they're in—if they want to get well. Do they want to be set free from sin? Do they want the joy I have for them?

When someone says yes, my child, I may very well send them your way. Listen as I guide you; be alert as I bring people across your path. I have placed you where you are for a reason. I want to give you the joy of ushering another beloved child into my kingdom.

**Read
John 5:1–18.**

*Show me who you've
sent me today, Lord.
Give me your words
to say.*

SEPTEMBER 15

I am the bread of life. —
John 6:35 (NKJV)

A SATISFIED SOUL

When my people wandered in the desert, I gave them bread to eat. They called it manna, the bread of heaven. I called it a symbol of the one I would send—my only Son.

My Son described himself as the bread of life, the one who can satisfy the deep hunger of the soul. I know your longings and desires, your wonderings about the future, the powerful temptation to satisfy your hunger with the things of this world.

Turn to me, loved one. I can satisfy every hunger, just as a loaf of bread, warm from the oven, can fill an empty stomach. When you feel hungry, my child—when your needs are great and the pangs are real—come to me. I alone can satisfy.

Read
John 6:22–40.

*Heavenly Father, I
choose to dine on all
that you have for me.*

SEPTEMBER 16

The right time for me has not yet come; for you any time is right.
—John 7:6 (NIV)

THE RIGHT TIME

Dear child, my perspective is different than yours. I can see all of time from beginning to end. I can view eternity. Meanwhile, your vision is limited to the present and the past.

In your limited view, you may think this is the right time for me to act. But my delay is not haphazard. I am waiting for the best possible moment to work on your behalf, to show my power in your circumstances. And I'm asking you to trust my timing.

I realize it can be excruciating to wait. But the waiting doesn't mean I love you any less. In fact, it's because of my love for you that I am carefully crafting a beautiful plan for your life.

Each piece of this magnificent design has not only a perfect place, but a perfect time—*my time.*

Read John 7:1–31.

Author of time, I trust you to work out your plan for my life in your perfect timing.

SEPTEMBER 17

*Let the one who has never
sinned throw the first stone!*
—**John 8:7** (NLT)

LEAVE JUDGMENT TO ME

The world is full of sin. It seems like at every turn you see people bent on corruption—disregarding my laws, acting deceitfully, behaving immorally.

Child, it is easy to point the finger at someone else's sin. It is tempting to condemn others for the evil they've done. But I urge you: don't be quick to judge. That is my job. I alone am holy. I alone can see into a person's heart. I alone know their motives.

I judge with wisdom and with justice. I judge with love. When I judge, I do not do it to point a finger or condemn. My desire is that everyone will come to me, repent, and turn from their sin.

Remember that I love *you* even when you fail and your behavior is less than perfect. Extend that love to others, and leave judgment to me.

Read
John 8:1–20.

*Righteous One, help me
to remember that you
alone are judge.*

SEPTEMBER 18

*You will know the truth, and
the truth will set you free.*
—**John 8:31–32** (HCSB)

SET FREE

Beloved, the world tries to tell you that you are free
only if you answer to no one but yourself. But this
is not true freedom, for your old self is enslaved to sin;
it answers to the whims of the flesh. When you trust in
me—*that's* when you become free. My words become part
of you. My Spirit gives you the strength to choose my
path. And sin loses its hold.

Hold to my teachings and you will find more than
deliverance from sin—you will find true freedom to be
who you were created to be. My teachings are really
an instruction book to a fulfilling, abundant life. From
them flow unrestrained joy and peace—a life brimming
with purpose. I do not fill your path with dreary do's
and don'ts; I give directions to a life unlimited by the
constraints of this world.

I offer to set you *free!*

**Read
John 8:31–59.**

*Author of liberty, help
me to follow your
instructions for a life
of freedom.*

This happened so that the work of God might be displayed in his life. —**John 9:3** (NIV)

MY GLORY IN YOU

Hardships. Pain. Suffering. Precious one, bring them all to me. I will gladly give you comfort. I will also make myself known in a way you've never seen before.

When my Son healed the blind man, my glory was revealed anew—to him and to all who knew him. For this reason, it is my delight to change pain into healing, joy into gloom, dark into light. So look to me with expectation. Look to me with hope. I can repurpose your pain to exhibit my care for you. I can use your suffering to show my healing power.

Dear one, I long to take away your pain and distress in a personal display of my glory. But your deliverance is for the sake of others too, for when you recognize and proclaim my work in your life, so will they. They will see my glory.

Read John 9:1–41.

Father, thank you for revealing yourself even in my pain.

The thief comes only to steal and kill and destroy; I came that they may have life; and have it abundantly. —**John 10:10** (NASB)

ABUNDANT LIFE

Dear one, some people will say that I have come to ruin the good life. They argue that my rules and restrictions kill all the fun. But child, nothing is farther from the truth. I want you to enjoy the most fulfilling life! I want your days to be filled with abundant joy!

It is because of my overflowing love for you that true joy is even possible. I don't offer you just a taste of happiness, a few morsels of excitement. I hold out *joy!* Joy everlasting that spills over from my heart to yours. Jubilation that floods your soul. Blessing that thrills your spirit and makes your heart soar.

Keep your ears tuned to my voice and your heart set on me. I won't let you down.

Read John 10:1–21.

Giver of all good gifts, thank you for offering a rich and satisfying life.

SEPTEMBER 21

I am the resurrection and the life. —**John 11:25** (NKJV)

BELIEVING THROUGH TEARS

Precious child, you wonder why I did not come, why I did not answer your prayer in the time you wanted in the way you wanted. Martha asked my Son the same question. She was disappointed that he did not immediately arrive to heal her brother. But as Jesus said to her, so I say to you in your situation: all hope did not die with your loved one.

Though death brings pain to those in its path, that pain will not last. I am the resurrection and the life. I conquered death so that you and all your loved ones may have eternal life—beyond the grave.

Like all mortals, you will die someday. But if you believe in me, you will live again. You may find this mystery hard to understand. Trust me anyway. Trust my words and take comfort, for this is my promise to you.

Read
John 11:1–32.

Lord, I believe in you. I know that your answer to my need will come in your perfect timing.

SEPTEMBER 22

Jesus, once more deeply moved, came to the tomb. It was a cave with a stone laid across the entrance. —**John 11:38** (NIV)

A PART OF LIFE

Emotions are a part of my being. I feel joy and gladness. I experience happiness and delight, love and compassion. But I am also deeply moved by your pain, and I grieve with you that the sin in the world has caused so much suffering.

Precious child, you can come to me with your feelings, whatever they are. I understand the tidal wave of emotions that engulf your spirit. I am aware of the ache in your soul. I recognize your hurting heart—for mine is bleeding too. I am full of tenderness and compassion for you.

Emotions are a part of life. You do not need to deny them or try to smother them. Bring me your heartaches and anger, your fear and sense of loss. Together we will grieve. Together we will mourn. And someday—together we will rejoice.

Read John 11:33–45.

Loving Father, thank you that you understand my joy and sorrow, happiness and pain.

Leave her alone. It was right for her to save this perfume for today, the day for me to be prepared for burial.

—John 12:7 (NCV)

EXTRAVAGANT GIFTS

Mary understood. She recognized that my Son's life here on earth was coming to a close, and she was moved to offer a rich, expensive gift. My heart was deeply touched by her extravagant offering—extravagant in cost and service. Mary was lavish in her love, unrestrained in her devotion. The scent of her perfume permeated the whole house. The fragrance of her life filled my heart.

I savor your devotion too, dear one. When your love spills out in sacrificial gifts, and your affection for me results in dedicated service, I am touched. Do not think your offerings go unnoticed. Like Mary's gift, your presents delight me—great or small—when they are given in faith and love. The fragrance of your devotion fills me with joy.

Read John 12:1–11.

Lord, I desire to give you extravagant gifts of love and service.

SEPTEMBER 24

Unless a kernel of wheat falls to the ground and dies, it remains only a single seed. But if it dies, it produces many seeds. —
John 12:24 (NIV)

DEATH PRODUCES LIFE

New life arises from the death of the old. Look at a seed. If you plant it, the water and the soil will work to destroy it. Yet only then will this single seed sprout and grow, producing many more seeds.

Look at my Son. My one and only Son died an excruciating physical death, but first he died to his own human desires so that you and many others could live.

Come to me for new life, dear one. If you can let go of things as they are now, I will sow a wealth of blessings into your life and bring about a harvest of new lives. And my kingdom will be multiplied.

Don't be afraid. Dying to worldly desires and human inclinations sounds like an exercise in futility, but it is exactly what produces life—*abundant life.*

Read John 12:20–36.

Lord, help me to die to my personal preferences and gain new life.

*I have come as light into the
world, so that everyone who
believes in me should not remain
in the darkness.*

—**John 12:46** (NRSV)

BASK IN MY LIGHT

Think about what it's like when you're sitting in a
dark room, and someone suddenly turns on the light.
You squint at first, but then you can see clearly, as if with
new eyes.

I offer you a far greater light—light for your soul. It's
a brilliance that casts the deepest darkness away. As you
trust in me, my brightness will illumine your life, lighting
up all the gloomy corners and revealing the path toward
me.

Sometimes you feel you are struggling in the dark,
groping to find your way. But take comfort and believe in
me. This is why I sent my Son to you—to be the light that
dispels the darkness.

My light will guide you, brighten your spirit, and
give you hope. Bask in the light.

Read
John 12:37–50.

*Light of the world,
brighten my soul.
I trust in you to light
my way.*

SEPTEMBER 26

I have given you an example, that you also should do just as I have done to you.

—**John 13:15** (ESV)

THE TRULY GREAT SERVE

Dear one, my own dear Son came to your world to serve, to do the most menial of tasks. He knew his position—Ruler over everything—yet that did not stop him from bending down to wash dirty feet. In profound love, he humbly stooped to serve.

As my child, you are also royalty—an heir of the King. But just as my Son gave up his greatness to serve, I am asking you to do the same. Be willing to bend down and take the lowly tasks. Be prepared to wait on others without their applause. Be ready to wrap a towel around your waist and get to work. As you take on ordinary tasks that no one else wants, I will notice. And I will bless you.

Those who are truly great serve. Be great, my child.

Read John 13:1–20.

Heavenly Father, thank you for your Son's willingness to serve. Help me to follow his example.

Your love for one another will prove to the world that you are my disciples. —**John 13:35** (NLT)

SUPERNATURAL LOVE

C hild, you belong to me. Nothing can change that. Now show the world that you are mine by loving my other children with your actions, not just your words.

My kind of love is far more than a feeling. It actively sets aside its own agenda to help others in need. It gives, sacrificing personal desires. It responds in kindness instead of anger. Follow my example and love others patiently, humbly, faithfully. Remember, you have my love—now extend it to others. Reach out, not only to those who respond with affection, but also to those who react with betrayal.

Others will notice this supernatural kind of love. They will recognize you are different. They will see that you belong to me.

Read
John 13:21–38.

Lord, help me to extend your love to others around me.

SEPTEMBER 28

I am the way, and the truth, and the life. No one comes to the Father except through me.
—**John 14:6** (ESV)

ONE WAY

Only one road leads to me; only one path goes through to heaven. My Son is the Way. I call out to the world to trust in his saving work and follow him.

Some people try to say that there are many roads to me, but I have lovingly prepared one path by which all may come. I have given the map in my Word. All one has to do is heed it.

The road is not difficult—in fact, I have done all the work; I have already paved the way. I only ask that people trust in what my Son has done and take the trail that he has blazed.

Jesus made it very clear—no one comes to me except through him. He is the Door, the Gate, the Way. With his sacrifice he has opened wide what had been closed by sin.

And that door leads into my loving arms.

**Read
John 14:1–14.**

Thank you for providing a way to you. I will follow your path.

I will not abandon you as orphans—I will come to you.
—**John 14:18** (NLT)

NEVER ALONE

You are my child. I will never abandon you, never leave you comfortless, helpless, or alone. I have sent my Spirit to live in you. I am with you wherever you go.

My Spirit acts as your counselor and advocate. He is a helper and a strengthener, an intercessor and a comforter. Everything you need to know, he will teach you. Every word you need to hear, he will bring to mind. Every comfort you need, he will provide.

My Spirit will pray for you when you don't have the words. He will guide you when you don't know the way. He will empower you when you don't have the strength to go one step farther.

Through him, I will give you peace—my own unique peace that does not disappear when trouble comes.

You are not now, not ever, alone.

Read
John 14:15–31.

Holy Spirit, thank you for your constant presence. Thank you for your comfort and strength.

SEPTEMBER 30

I am the vine, you are the branches. —**John 15:5** (NKJV)

THE ULTIMATE TEAM

Your life is filled with activity, your calendar filled with things to do. Still, your heart's desire is to be my faithful and obedient servant—and that brings me joy.

My child, this fruit you are looking for, the goals you are pursuing—don't forget that they come through my sustaining power. As a branch can only produce fruit when connected to the vine, so you can only make a spiritual impact in this world through me. We are in this together.

So today, take some time to simply rest in me. Draw your strength from me. In prayer, in reading, perhaps in just taking a break from the bustle, turn your heart toward me. I'll provide everything you need for the next segment of the journey.

Read John 15:1–17.

Loving Father, I give these tasks to you and seek your power to keep going.

OCTOBER

OCTOBER 1

You are not of the world . . .
I chose you out of the world,
therefore the world hates you.
—**John 15:19** (ESV)

BECAUSE YOU'RE SPECIAL

Beloved, out of my love for you, I have chosen you
to walk a different path. Putting your trust in my
Son means that you do not walk according to the ways of
the world. The lightness of your step and your joy in the
journey—gifts of my Spirit—cause you to stand out.

Don't let the opinions of those who doubt me cause
you to question your uniqueness or my deep love for you.
The enemy of your soul cannot stand the hope that I offer
the world through you. He will try to discourage you or
cause you to conform to the world's image, but he will fail.

You, beloved, bear my fragrance. You are my image.
Know that I am always with you and will always protect
you.

Read
John 15:18—16:4.

When I'm tempted to
conform to the world,
remind me that I am
yours.

OCTOBER 2

Until now you have asked for nothing in My name. Ask and you will receive, that your joy may be complete. —**John 16:24**
(HCSB)

THE PATH TO JOY

My child, you can ask me, your heavenly Father, for anything. Because I delight to give you good gifts, I invite you to come before me with an expectant heart.

My desire is for you to have the kind of abundant, contagious joy that overflows like a fountain and causes those you meet to sense my presence. The kind that springs up in your heart and waters your soul. The kind that comes through my Spirit when he reminds you of my promises and abiding love.

Keep turning to me in prayer, beloved. Ask and you will receive.

Read
John 16:13–33.

Joy. I want and need it so badly in my life. Help me find it in you alone.

OCTOBER 3

As You sent Me into the world,
I also have sent them into the
world. —**John 17:18** (NKJV)

SHARE THE JOY

I have watched your eyes light up when you received a great gift. You joyously shared the news, knowing that others would want to join in your delight.

My child, I have given a great gift to the world— eternal forgiveness through the death of my Son. Never again will you and I be separated. This is the free gift of my love—one that only requires acceptance. It also comes with a bonus: everlasting life with me and an inheritance beyond your wildest dreams.

Just as my Son sent his disciples, I am sending you, beloved, to share the joy of this gift. But I do not send you alone. I will go with you and strengthen you.

Read
John 17.

Strengthen me, Lord,
as I take your light into
the world.

Mary Magdalene went and announced to the disciples, "I have seen the Lord!"

—**John 20:18** (HCSB)

HE IS ALIVE!

My child, I have good news for you: I have conquered death! My Son's empty tomb is proof of that.

Jesus' friends and disciples felt deep sorrow at his death, and again when the stone was rolled against his tomb. It was like an arrow, piercing them to the core and shredding their peace. What a contrast on the day he rose again! The joy on Mary's face when she recognized him was sweet to behold. Jesus' resurrection showed that I keep my promises and that my power knows no bounds.

It is also a reminder that even though you pass through the deep waters of sorrow, you will not drown. Death no longer has the victory, child. Because my Son lives, so will you.

Read
John 20:1–18.

Lord, like Mary, I long to behold you. I look forward to the day when I will.

OCTOBER 5

Put your finger here and see
my hands. Reach out your hand
and put it in my side. Do not
doubt but believe.

—**John 20:27** (NRSV)

FROM DOUBT TO BELIEF

You are my treasured creation. I know every hidden
quality within you. And what I love the most is when
you are absolutely honest with me, relating doubts, fears,
frustrations and all—openly.

I yearn to take you on a journey, my child, from
doubt to belief. The journey begins when you rest your
questions in my capable hands. Truly, you can put aside
the fear that I will chide you for having doubts. That is
not who I am. My heart is to offer you a fresh revelation
of my presence instead.

My Son knew that Thomas's faith needed the
strengthening his presence provided. Doubts fled in the
face of pure love and the evidence of nail-scarred hands.

So go ahead, ask your questions—and watch those
doubts scatter.

Read
John 20:19 — 21:14.

Help me to be honest
and real in my
relationship with you.

OCTOBER 6

If I want him to remain alive
until I return, what is that
to you? As for you, follow me.
—**John 21:22** (NLT)

LOOK TO ME

Well done, beloved! You have been doing an
incredible job! I am so proud of your willingness
to serve me—the many ways in which you have stepped
out to declare my praises in often hostile environments.
Your deep love and passionate desire to serve me make
me glad.

Rest in the fullness of my approval, child. When
the temptation to compare yourself with others beckons,
don't give in to the enemy's schemes. He seeks to distract
you and lead you astray, onto his path. A path full of
heartache, fear, and resentment.

Instead, follow where I lead and keep your eyes on
me. My eyes are always lovingly on you.

Read
John 21:15–25.

I fix my eyes on you
and you alone, O Lord.

OCTOBER 7

You will receive power when the Holy Spirit has come upon you, and you will be my witnesses. —**Acts 1:8** (ESV)

MY POWER IS IN YOU

My child, my offer of the Holy Spirit's power stands for all times—not just the first century. My Spirit is the fire that still ignites the body of Christ. Through him, I offer you the power to help change a world starved for good news.

Be filled with my Spirit, beloved. The words you speak and the actions you take on behalf of my Son will be drenched with power and saturated with life, because I will speak and act through you. You don't have to "feel" powerful; in faith I work through you, regardless.

As you dedicate yourself to me, there is no limit to what I can accomplish through you.

Read
Acts 1:1–11.

Lord, give me the confidence to believe your Holy Spirit is working through me.

OCTOBER 8

Lord, you know everyone's
heart. Show us which one of
these two you have chosen.
—**Acts 1:24** (NIV)

I CAN HELP YOU

No matter how small the situation may seem to you, I am always delighted when you turn to me for guidance. Come to me with your decisions big and small, child. I care about every one of them and want to guide you to make the best choices.

Use the tools I have given to help you: my Word, my Spirit, and my wisdom. My Spirit will lead you into all truth and will confirm my will through my Word, just as he did for my disciples.

You can know my will, my choices. My Word and my Spirit will never lead you astray.

Read
Acts 1:12-26.

Lord, I invite your
guidance into all my
decisions.

OCTOBER 9

Utterly amazed, they asked: "Are not all these men who are speaking Galileans?"

—**Acts 2:7** (NLT)

I CAN DO ANYTHING THROUGH YOU

I delight to amaze people. And there is no limit to my ability to do so. After all, my mercies are new each morning. I work miracles that shatter expectations—that turn "How can this be?" into praise.

My Son's disciples always went against the grain. While some people saw only uneducated fisherman, I saw fishers of men who brought great honor to my Son. Likewise, sweet child, some may discount your abilities and desires and cause you to see only limitations to what you can do. But I can do anything—*anything*—through you.

Read
Acts 2:1–13.

God, I offer myself to be used by you anywhere, and in any way.

OCTOBER 10

Peter stood up with the Eleven, raised his voice and addressed the crowd. —**Acts 2:14** (NIV)

A TURNAROUND LIFE

B eloved, I share the joy of parents eager to talk about their children. Look at my son, Peter. Like you, he is special to me.

Once, Peter could not see beyond the shame of denying my Son. But one mistake does not define a life, nor does one blunder destroy it. Peter's usefulness to me was not over. Instead, it had just begun. His denial was the kernel of wheat that would fall to the ground and reap a harvest of blessing.

This is the beauty of my grace. It takes a person from pain to purpose. So know that I still love you. I am a grace-filled and grace-giving God. Hope for a new beginning can turn your life around. I did it for Peter. I will do it for you.

Read
Acts 2:14–41.

Loving God, forgive me for the times when I deny you. Restore me once again.

OCTOBER 11

*In the name of Jesus Christ of
Nazareth, rise up and walk.*
—Acts 3:6 (NKJV)

BEYOND EXPECTATIONS

I know the expectations of the world—what it deems
worthwhile or valuable. Many seek silver or gold—like
the poor man at the Beautiful Gate—believing that money
is the answer to their problems. Others seek approval from
those they esteem, hoping it will give meaning to their
broken lives. But what I offer is beyond price, beyond a
quick fix, and often beyond preconceived notions. I offer
you my Spirit. My Son already paid the price.

Through the gift of my Spirit, you can have life and
wholeness in place of your brokenness, crippled attitudes,
and stunted growth. I offer you joy in the face of your
worst sorrow.

Rise up, child. Walk in faith.

Read
Acts 2:42 – 3:10.

*Lord, I want what
you want for my life.
I receive all that you
offer.*

OCTOBER 12

Why do you stare at us as if
by our own power or godliness
we had made this man walk?
—**Acts 3:12** (NIV)

BEYOND THE VEIL

My child, I still open the eyes of the blind and make the lame walk. Many times, I perform these great works through human hands because of the joy of involving my people. But each act serves to draw people to me.

While Peter and John knew that I was the source of their display of power, others could see only the men I used. Only with faith and the conviction of my Spirit do you see beyond the veil and into the light of heaven.

Dear one, I am honored when you point the way toward me and resist the urge to retain the spotlight. Through your humility I am exalted.

Read
Acts 3:11 — 4:4.

God, you alone deserve
all the credit.

OCTOBER 13

*When they saw the courage of
Peter and John ... they took note
that these men had been with
Jesus.* —**Acts 4:13** (NIV)

CONNECTED TO ME

Just as a good father delights when others see the
resemblance between him and his children, so I delight
to see the resemblance between my children and my Son
Jesus.

Like Jesus, Peter and John were boundless in their
faith and powerful in their walk. People were amazed at
their influence and power. What they lacked, they found
in me. My Spirit, my presence, invigorated their walk.
Their relationship with me made the difference.

Time spent with me will make the difference in your
life as well, beloved. Live close to me. Stay connected to
the vine—my Son. His gentleness and grace will fill you,
giving you the courage to stand—and the strength to make
a difference.

**Read
Acts 4:5–22.**

*Lord, I want to
experience your
presence each moment
of this day.*

OCTOBER 14

And now, O Lord, hear their threats, and give us, your servants, great boldness in preaching your word. —**Acts 4:29** (NLT)

BOLDNESS TO WITNESS

My Spirit makes all the difference, child. I gave Peter and John great courage to witness despite the threats against them. The onslaught of attacks did not silence them; instead, the opposition fueled their courage and desire to spread the message of my Son.

If you ask, I will give you boldness to speak on my behalf. Will you speak?

My Spirit indwells you, dear one. You are the recipient of forgiveness—my great message of hope. You are my mouthpiece, the purveyor of grace to others. Tell them about my wonder-working power and my gift, which was bought by my precious Son. Be bold today.

Read Acts 4:23-31.

Boldly I go forth into my world this day to speak for you.

OCTOBER 15

Barnabas . . . sold a field that belonged to him and brought the money and laid it at the apostles' feet. —Acts 4:36–37 (ESV)

GENUINE GENEROSITY

B eloved, when you take notice of the poor, the widowed, and the orphaned, you bring me glory. When you give to those who are friendless and without means, you are giving to me also.

The generosity of my son Barnabas had the fragrance of my Spirit. He chose to give out of love, not out of obligation or a desire to gain something in return. Truly, this is the very essence of laying up treasure in heaven.

My child, come to me with your desire to give, as well as any fears of giving. Let me be your partner. I can fill a shrinking heart with so much love and compassion that giving becomes a pleasure, not a regret. A privilege, not a burden.

Try me and see as we give together.

Read
Acts 4:32–5:11.

O Lord, fill my heart with generosity and compassion.

OCTOBER 16

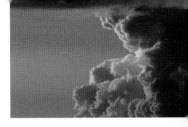

The apostles left the council and were happy, because God had considered them worthy to suffer for the sake of Jesus.

—**Acts 5:41** (CEV)

REJOICE IN THE JOURNEY

My dear child, when you walk the dark path of suffering, you bring great honor to my Son. All of heaven rejoices as you take a stand in his name.

My Son was despised and abused. In humility, he left the splendor of heaven to come to earth, knowing that he would walk the path of shame and disgrace. But he chose the greater cause—to save my people—rather than to save himself. Forever he will bear the marks from the cross. Those marks are badges of honor given to all who suffer for the sake of righteousness.

Child, to be sure, bearing my Son's name means you also walk the same path and bear the same marks. But there is much blessing in the journey, for I am here, close beside you.

Read
Acts 5:12–42.

Help me, Father, to rejoice when I endure suffering for your name.

OCTOBER 17

Select from among you seven men of good reputation, full of the Spirit and wisdom, whom we can appoint to this duty.
—Acts 6:3–4 (HCSB)

A VITAL PART

In the body of believers you play a crucial role. Do not be afraid or intimidated. I have equipped you with abilities to do that for which I call you. No gift that I give is insignificant. I have blessed you with power through the Holy Spirit. I am here to give you confidence through prayer.

Precious one, all tasks within my kingdom bear the stamp of my call—full of my Spirit and wisdom. As with my gifts, no task is insignificant. I am pleased with your good reputation, your acts of service. Washing the feet of a tired man, giving food to a widow, or preaching a sermon are of equal importance to me. All are necessary for building up the body of Christ. All are applauded in heaven.

Read
Acts 6.

I'm on board with your plans, God! Just tell me what to do!

OCTOBER 18

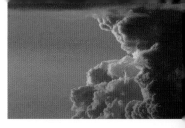

Look, I see the heavens opened and the Son of Man standing in the place of honor at God's right hand! —**Acts 7:56** (NLT)

YOU WILL SEE ME

I have promised that the pure in heart will see me. In the last moments of his life on earth, my precious son Stephen caught sight of my glory. Although his suffering was real, I helped him through that darkness and into my light. My Son Jesus stood to welcome him into my presence.

Many have suffered or died as a result of worshiping me. No less than you, they are of infinite worth to me. Their last moments were spent sheltered under my wings, protected by my Spirit. Though they died, yet do they live, and so it will be with you also. When you pass through the waters of death, dear one, my Son will be there to welcome you Home.

R e a d
A c t s   7 : 3 0 – 6 0 .

Lord, thank you for your promise to welcome me into heaven.

OCTOBER 19

The believers who were scattered preached the Good News about Jesus wherever they went.
—Acts 8:4 (NLT)

A SPECIAL ASSIGNMENT

Precious child, I hear your prayers and see how burdened you are over an uncertain future. Trusting me when you don't know where that road is leading can be a challenge. But you honor me when you persevere through all things.

In the days of the early church I used persecution to promote the spread of the gospel message. Likewise, I can use the seemingly insurmountable roadblocks in your life to accomplish great things for my kingdom.

Don't let the worries of today stop you from pressing on tomorrow. Keep praying. Draw near to me through my Word. And know that I am boldly forging a way through the roadblocks.

Read
Acts 8:1–25.

These times are hard and I don't see where we're going, but I will trust you anyway.

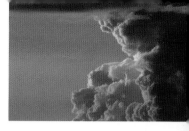

OCTOBER 20

Philip began to speak, and starting with this same Scripture, he told the man the Good News about Jesus. —**Acts 8:35** (NCV)

SPREAD THE WORD

Your passionate desire to see others brought into the same kind of loving relationship that you and I share brings me so much joy. Yet I know that you sometimes feel inadequate in telling others about my Son. But fear not—I go before you and am actively working in people's lives, preparing their hearts. When I lead them to you, you will be surprised at how your willingness to direct a conversation to spiritual matters can lead to deep conversations about me.

Everyone needs me, whether they can verbalize it yet or not. Deep down, they can sense their separation from me. Without my Son, they can never cross that chasm; but with him, new life awaits!

Be bold and courageous as you reach out with this message of hope and life.

Read
Acts 8:26–40.

Give me boldness and courage as I share the gospel with those nearest to me.

OCTOBER 21

*A light from heaven flashed
around him. And falling to the
ground he heard a voice . . .*
—Acts 9:3–4 (ESV)

HEAVEN CALLING

I call my children in so many ways. For some, like
Saul, a dramatic encounter on a public road was
needed. For others, a wooing whisper to the heart is all
it takes to bring them into fellowship with me. My sheep
know my voice.

My call on your life is as absolute as it was on Saul's.
Your conversion is just as important to me as his was. I
called Saul to give up his life for the sake of my kingdom.
I call you to do the same—to give up your life to me and
let me give it back in fullness and joy.

You were created to go and do amazing things for my
kingdom.

Read
Acts 9:1–19.

*Heavenly Father, I offer
you my heart and life.*

OCTOBER 22

Barnabas accepted Saul and took him to the apostles.

—Acts 9:27 (NCV)

THE ENCOURAGER

I take great delight in the expansion of my kingdom. The entire universe is pulsing with joy over the growing community of believers. And you, loved one, have an exciting part to play.

You are my Barnabas—my encouraging one. As I create a new people for myself, as I bring in the harvest, you can encourage those young in the faith. You don't need special training or extensive knowledge to be an encourager; it just takes time and love. I filled you with my Spirit that you might pour out my love into the lives of others.

Together, let's encourage and build up those who've just joined our family!

Read
Acts 9:20–31.

Grant me, Lord, the right words to encourage others.

She was always doing kind things for others and helping the poor. —**Acts 9:36** (NLT)

POWER IN KINDNESS

I am overjoyed when you do kind things for others. Tabitha spent her time making robes and clothing for the poor. I long for you to reach out in similar ways to help those in need.

Tabitha's reputation for kindness caused those close to her to seek that she be brought back to life—and so they sent for Peter! Imagine such faith! I honored that simple yet profound faith by granting her friends' request.

Many in your world can use a touch of kindness. All around you are people who need the help that you can offer. The gifts and abilities you have will build my kingdom. Just place them in my hands and let me show you who needs you.

Read
Acts 9:32–43.

O Great Physician, I'm grateful for your encouragement to bring the needs of loved ones to you.

OCTOBER 24

Cornelius . . . was divinely directed by a holy angel to call you to his house and to hear a message from you.

—**Acts 10:22** (HCSB)

IN MOTION

There are no coincidences in life, dear one. I work in unexpected ways to set just the right people in positions where they can do the greatest good. As I work, I consider all possible avenues and confirm my Word, just as I did for Peter and Cornelius. I always work all things together for good.

I still direct my people in ways that fulfill my will too. That sudden thought to pray for a friend or send an encouraging message to a family member is part of a plan I've already set in motion to bring about a good result. It is my delight, child, to work with you to build my kingdom.

Read
Acts 10:1–23.

God, you show yourself to those who truly seek you.

God shows no favoritism. In every nation he accepts those who fear him and do what is right. —**Acts 10:34–35** (NLT)

BUILDING BRIDGES

You are greatly loved, child. And the love I have never divides, never excludes. It builds bridges across all man-made barriers.

I called my son Peter to visit a man whose home he otherwise would never have entered. In such a way, beloved, I call you to love others—to be a bridge-builder to all your neighbors, not just the ones next door. They do not look exactly like you or speak as you do. They may live halfway around the world, with no concept of my love. But they are your neighbors nonetheless, just as much as those who live on your block.

Together we can build a bridge to them all—one that will withstand the floodwaters of hate and misunderstanding that the enemy of your souls likes to send.

Come, my child. Let us show the world that I do not play favorites. All are welcome.

Read Acts 10:24–48.

Lord, I want to be a bridge-builder. Grant me the wisdom and the knowledge to do so.

OCTOBER 26

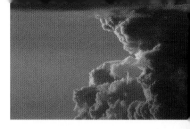

They glorified God, saying,
"So God has granted repentance
resulting in life to even the
Gentiles!" —**Acts 11:18** (HCSB)

MY IN-CROWD

There is no boundary to my love—there are no insiders or outsiders. The only requirement for entry into my kingdom is acceptance of the death of my Son, Jesus Christ, on one's behalf. My invitation is so open that even those you imagine won't ever come to me are invited to my table to feast with me for eternity.

Be a courageous peacemaker, beloved. Do not allow the seeds of division to take root in your heart and branch out to others. Instead, preach the Good News. Tell the world that my in-crowd includes anyone who will come to me.

Read
Acts 11:1–18.

Lord, please grant me
the boldness to share
Jesus with everyone
around me.

OCTOBER 27

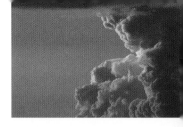

*She was so overjoyed that,
instead of opening the gate, she
ran in and announced that
Peter was standing at the gate.*
—Acts 12:14 (NRSV)

I WILL ANSWER YOUR PRAYERS

Beloved, I love to surprise you with my bounty—an
abundant answer to what you believe is an
impossible prayer. I am the God who can do anything. I
love to watch your face light up and hear the gladness in
your voice as you relay my answers to others.

I answer each prayer in my own time, in accordance
with my will. While not every prayer for that "impossible"
request will be answered in the way you hope, every
prayer *is* answered. I always have the best good in mind
for you and for those about whom you pray. So do not fret
or believe the lie that I answer some prayers and disregard
others. All your prayers will be answered.

**Read
Acts 12:1–17.**

*Lord, I praise you
for the blessing of
answered prayer.*

OCTOBER 28

*Dedicate Barnabas and Saul
for the special work to which
I have called them.*

—Acts 13:2 (NLT)

SEND THEM TO THE WORLD

Child of mine, I created you for community and I
know how much you love those who are closest
to you. These brothers and sisters within the body of
believers are some of your most trusted friends and
counselors. But community was never meant to be
hoarded, never meant to remain static. I made it fluid, to
change as needs arise and my call directs you elsewhere.

I bring people together for a time to allow iron to
sharpen iron. Saying good-bye is never easy. Pray for
your friends, and pray for yourself. I will be with you and,
just as I have done so many times before, I will give you
strength and peace through it all.

**Read
Acts 13:1–12.**

*It pains me to see those
closest to me move
away. Please help me to
get through this, Lord.*

OCTOBER 29

*We are men also, with the same
nature as you, and we are
proclaiming good news to you.*
—**Acts 14:15** (HCSB)

I AM THE LIVING GOD

I am who I am, my child. I bring forth the
constellations in their seasons. I know when and
where the mountain goat gives birth. I am served by the
wild ox and give the horse his strength. Yet many who
walk under my sun attribute my works to other gods—
ones they think they recognize or believe they can find
at little cost to themselves. They see gods they can fully
understand and predict. I see people lost in darkness and
in need of my light. Will you go to them?

I have given you the gift of my presence and the
power of my Spirit. Together, let's find those who are lost
and bring them into my marvelous light.

**Read
Acts 14:1–18.**

*Lord, protect me from
idolatry and point my
heart toward you and
you alone.*

*Therefore my judgment is that
we should not trouble those of
the Gentiles who turn to God.*
—**Acts 15:19** (ESV)

BE GRACIOUS

As the God who zealously and tirelessly pursues
each individual, it grieves me to see the burdens
placed on others under the guise of pleasing me. Instead
of honoring my true commands, people make assumptions
into yokes that burden the faithful and drive the lost away
from me. But, beloved, my commands are not burdensome
or legalistic. My yoke is easy and my grace sufficient for
every need. I readily give grace to the humble and have
compassion on those in need.

Let your conversation be gracious, child. Soothe the
wounded with your words of peace and hope. Encourage,
exhort, and extend my grace to others.

Read
Acts 15:1–21.

*Father, help me to
show grace to those I
am working with.*

They had such a sharp disagreement that they parted company. —**Acts 15:39** (NIV)

SERVING THROUGH DISAGREEMENT

Sometimes people have to agree to disagree, my child. I know that it can be confusing when my people, called by my name, saved by my Son, have differences of opinion about earthly matters. Barnabas and Paul were at odds over my servant John Mark, and they could not immediately resolve their differences.

In the midst of that difficult situation, I was at work, turning their disagreement into two missionary efforts, not just one. The goal, always, is to grow my kingdom. My servants agreed on that point and continued on that task.

Differences will occur. Seek me when they do. Let me guide you. I will show you the way I want you to walk.

Read Acts 15:22–41.

Lord, give me wisdom when I face disagreements with my brothers and sisters in Christ.

NOVEMBER

The churches were strengthened in the faith and grew daily in numbers. —**Acts 16:5** (NIV)

STRENGTHENED IN THE FAITH

Your every step of obedience, though it may not seem like much to you, has eternal impact in my kingdom here on earth. Your light shines brightly in a dark world. People are being drawn to my Son as they see him powerfully at work in your life.

Keep going, child. Keep loving those who are lost. Keep showing compassion for those in need. Keep meeting with other believers and encouraging them in their faith. Most of all, keep coming to me for spiritual nourishment and growth. Through you, I will strengthen and grow my family.

With my loving Spirit, even your smallest efforts can yield amazing results. Remember that a little becomes much in my hands.

Read Acts 16:1–15.

Equip me, Father, to strengthen others in the faith, that your church might increase.

NOVEMBER 2

Around midnight Paul and Silas were praying and singing hymns to God, and the other prisoners were listening.

—Acts 16:25 (NLT)

I WILL HEAR

My child, I know that life is often difficult. When you suffer ill health, experience tight finances, face strained relationships or hardships because of your belief in me, I feel everything that you feel. I am there with you in the pain of seemingly insurmountable problems; I am present in the strain of everyday struggles—strengthening you with my grace so that you can overcome every obstacle.

As Paul and Silas did for the other prisoners in the dungeon, let others see the difference my power makes in your adversity. Difficulties are a part of life, but your response to them will help someone else find me. Others will see that my power enables you to face difficulties with prayer instead of panic, with calm assurance instead of fear, with joy instead of despair, and with hymns of praise instead of laments. Then they will clamor to know the One who can make all of that possible—me.

Read Acts 16:16–40.

Father, may my response to every struggle display trust in your grace.

The Bereans . . . searched the Scriptures day after day to see if Paul and Silas were teaching the truth. —**Acts 17:11** (NLT)

MY LOVE LETTER

I applaud your search for truth and meaning. I gave you an inquisitive mind—one that refuses to accept an opinion purely at face value but keeps searching for truth. I have written a beautiful book with you in mind. In this volume, I tell the breathtaking story of my Son's sacrifice for you and his miraculous defeat over your greatest enemies—Satan and death. I explain my amazing plans for your life and direct you on the best path to achieve your purpose.

Study this book, for my words give life, wisdom, and guidance. As you eagerly examine the Scriptures, you will see my love more clearly. You will better understand my kingdom and my purpose for your life.

I long to spend time with you daily. Read and reread my love letters to you. Listen as I speak to you with grace and wisdom.

Read Acts 17:1–15.

Author of Scripture, thank you for your life-giving words of love, grace, and wisdom.

NOVEMBER 4

[Paul] reasoned in the synagogue with the Jews and the God fearing Greeks, as well as in the marketplace.

—Acts 17:17 (NIV)

HELD SECURE

A tent held securely by tent pegs does not flap about in the breeze; it remains securely grounded. This is my plan for you, my child. Your life could be like that tent, buffeted by the winds of others' opinions . . . except that I have a better plan.

I want you to be so grounded in the truth of my Son—the firm foundation of your faith—that when others challenge you, you will not be blown about by vain philosophies. Instead, your words and convictions will be ones I provided through my Spirit.

With this foundation, no one will be able to move you from your position of faith. But *you* will move others by the power of my Spirit.

**Read
Acts 17:16–34.**

Father, I'm grateful to the Holy Spirit for keeping me secure in your truth.

NOVEMBER 5

*A solemn fear descended on
the city, and the name of the
Lord Jesus was greatly honored.*
—Acts 19:17 (NLT)

NAME ABOVE ALL NAMES

I delight to hear you honor me in worship. I rejoice in your desire to bring honor to my Son in whatever you do. When you honor him, you honor me.

The name of my Son carries my full authority and blessing. We are one in this. When you call on him, you call on me. In his name you are forgiven. In his name you are baptized into new life. In his name you are rescued from evil. Demons flee at the mention of his name. At his name every knee in heaven and on earth will bow.

Child, the name of my Son brings you directly to me. Speak his name, and I will answer.

**Read
Acts 19:1–22.**

*Name above all names,
help me to use your
name with honor and
respect.*

NOVEMBER 6

*During that time, there was
some serious trouble in Ephesus
about the Way of Jesus.*

—**Acts 19:23** (NCV)

MY WAY

Beloved, I set you on a path straight to me. My road
directs you to joy and purpose. As you travel on my
road, be alert to distractions that cause you to wander
off-course.

My followers have always faced difficulty, for my
way is narrow and few choose to walk in it. But you have
chosen my way, precious one. You have decided to take
the narrow path, to stay close beside me, to walk in my
footsteps. When you're that close, my child, you never
have to worry about getting lost or going the wrong
direction. I will guide you. Even as troubles arise, I will
be with you.

**Read
Acts 19:23–41.**

*Father, help me to
show others the true
Way—the path to life
and truth.*

NOVEMBER 7

*While there, [Paul] encouraged
the believers in all the towns he
passed through.*

—**Acts 20:2** (NLT)

FRESH HOPE

Come to me daily, beloved, for a fresh supply of
hope and strength. Everyday problems can drain
your reserves. But I offer you new hope every morning.
Be confident of my love, assured of my power, and
strengthened to confront each day's problems.

Many around you face discouragement and
disappointments. Some are desperate and drained of
hope. As you come before me, seeking a measure of my
grace, I will open your eyes to the plight of others. Be
my instrument, child, of courage and hope. I will help you
soar like an eagle and, in turn, lift those who are bound.

**Read
Acts 20:1–12.**

*Giver of hope, thank
you for your gift of
encouragement. I will
pass it on today.*

NOVEMBER 8

My life is worth nothing to me unless I use it for finishing the work assigned me by the Lord Jesus. —**Acts 20:24** (NLT)

JUST BREATHE

Dear one, all runners require enough breath to stay in the race set before them. I am the breath of life. I will give you the endurance to run your race until the end.

You breathe in and out each day without conscious thought. That's trust. I desire that same trust as you run the course I've established for you. Trust in my ability to help you live this life well and to complete the work I have begun in you. Trust in my grace to guide you through temptation, fear, and doubt.

As you run, invigorated with my love and grace, others will be encouraged in their race. Breathe in my strength. Breathe out fear. Keep yours eyes on me—and head for the finish. Your prize is waiting.

Read
Acts 20:13–38.

Father, please help me keep my eye on the finish line. I commit to completing my assignment.

NOVEMBER 9

I am ready not only to be bound,
but also to die in Jerusalem
for the name of the Lord Jesus.
—**Acts 21:13** (NIV)

READINESS

You are so precious to me that I gave up my own Son's life for you. I sacrificed what was most dear so that you and I could spend eternity together.

Paul's trust in me was a sacrifice so richly fragrant, you can still smell its sweetness thousands of years later. Its aroma came from the knowledge of my Son and the power of his name. Paul was ready to face suffering because he knew what lay ahead: the glory of his inheritance.

Child, I promise to reward you with much more than you will ever sacrifice in this life. Release your grip on the things you think you cannot hand over to me. When you give me your whole life, you will experience a freedom you have never known.

Read
Acts 21:1-16.

Lord, I place every
part of my life in your
loving hands.

NOVEMBER 10

Everyone who heard this praised God.

—**Acts 21:20** (CEV)

OVERFLOWING WITH PRAISE

Some responses are automatic. A balloon filled with air inflates. A river filled with water overflows. A heart filled with my Spirit delights to see good triumph. And good will triumph, child. Believe that.

I am still at work, drawing new people to me across the globe. But I also reach out to the citizens of your country and work in the lives of your neighbors. So fill your mind with what is good and true—and encourage others to do the same. When you do, your hearts will expand with joy.

Paul praised my work because his heart was filled with my Spirit. Let my good news and my Spirit fill your heart with joy.

Read
Acts 21:17–34.

Spirit, I praise you for your work in changing hearts around the world.

NOVEMBER 11

"Brothers and esteemed fathers,"
Paul said, "listen to me as I
offer my defense."

—**Acts 22:1** (NLT)

OUR LOVE STORY

Dear one, good news is powerful. So powerful that it blesses both the messenger and his or her listeners.

How I love to hear you tell the story of our meeting, of the moment you discovered my love for you! When you share about my grace in your life, another person may draw closer to me. Your words of how you became my child may help someone else join my family.

Eloquence is not essential. Simply talk about how you needed me and how I changed your life. Speak of my power and my peace. Your straightforward and honest account of my presence in your life will make a difference.

How I love our love story.

Read
Act 22:1–21.

Lord, thank you for changing my life. Help me to share our love story.

*The prisoner, Paul, asked me
to bring this young man to you.
He wants to tell you something.*
—Acts 23:17 (NCV)

NO SMALL JOBS

There are many people at work in my kingdom. Some work before crowds, preaching the deeds of my Son before kings. Others work behind the scenes in quiet ways. All have a voice; all are used by my Spirit to bring life.

Paul's nephew is mentioned only briefly in Scripture, but in my big picture, a "little" task like his can have big results. His availability and willingness to speak up before the Roman commander saved Paul's life.

My child, no job in my kingdom is ever too small. I have special tasks for you and you alone. So do what you've been given to do. I will bless your willingness to complete your task with the power of my Spirit.

**Read
Acts 22:30 – 23:22.**

*Lord, I am willing.
Do with me what you
wish.*

NOVEMBER 13

*Provide horses for Paul to ride,
and get him safely to Governor
Felix.* —**Acts 23:24** (NLT)

YOUR DEFENDER

Do not fear if you are wrongly accused, and do not
pay attention to the circumstances that surround
you. Instead, look to me. I will defend you. My strength
will sustain you. My righteous right hand will uphold you.

Because I am sovereign, I can turn the hearts and
minds of all those who have misjudged you, just as I
did for Paul. The captain, the governor, and even the
prosecuting attorney did only what I allowed them to do
in Caesarea that day.

I helped Paul; I will help you. I am your Father,
and you are my child. Know that I love you, and am
committed to protecting you. All I ask is that you trust
me enough to let me do it.

**Read
Acts 23:23 — 24:27.**

*My great, glorious
Father, I'm so glad
you fight for me!*

NOVEMBER 14

I am not guilty of any crime against the Jewish laws or the Temple or the Roman government. —**Acts 25:8** (NLT)

STAND STRONG

L amb of mine, the hurtful accusations of others are a sad consequence of a fallen world. As my Son promised, persecution is the province of those who belong to my family. When you are devastated by accusing words, remember that I hear them too and feel your anguish. Come to me and lift your hurting heart heavenward. I will apply my healing balm to your wounds. I will help you hold your head up and declare your innocence as I did for Paul when he stood before Festus.

Be comforted in knowing that I will never allow my purposes for your life's work to be thwarted. I am your God, and I will defend you.

Read
Acts 25:1–22.

How safe I feel, God, knowing you are my defender.

Agrippa said to Paul, "You almost persuade me to become a Christian."

—**Acts 26:28** (NKJV)

ALMOST PERSUADED

As you speak of me to those around you and they still remain unconvinced, you may wonder if more effort on your part or mine would have made the difference. Don't give way to frustration. Remember, I know the human heart. Because I would never break a bruised reed or snuff out a smoldering wick, I choose to persuade rather than push.

Agrippa chose to hold on to his perceptions rather than relinquish all to follow me. He pitied my son Paul, who stood before him in chains, unaware that Paul was the one who was really free.

My child, to *almost* persuade is to faithfully plant seeds in that person's life. In my timing, those seeds will be watered and, by my grace, will bear fruit.

Read Acts 26.

Lord, let me never be discouraged but continue to speak for you.

Last night an angel came to me from the God I belong to and worship. —Acts 27:23 (NCV)

MY POSSESSION

Loved one, you are my most prized possession. You are always in my thoughts and forever in my heart. I have counted every hair on your head and deemed you of infinite worth. I value all who belong to me and deliver them when they are in trouble. I may not always send an angel, as I did for Paul. I may choose instead to work through the quiet word of a friend, or through a spouse who reminds you of my love for you. But I will deliver you.

When you find yourself in an impossible storm, call on me. I may give you a plan of action, send you a word of encouragement, or come to your aid. In any case, I will always watch over and protect you.

Read
Acts 27:1–26.

Heavenly Father, thank you for watching over me in the storms.

NOVEMBER 17

The others held onto planks or debris from the broken ship. So everyone escaped safely to shore. —**Acts 27:44** (NLT)

ALWAYS SAFE

My child, when the storms of this life—figurative or literal—sweep through, I know the helplessness you feel. In the wake of their destructive force, you wonder why I would allow such upheaval. Yet you are always safe with me.

I allow storms so that you may experience my presence in ways you would not know otherwise. The waves in your life may be high and you may be frightened. But if you will stay in the haven of my protection—just as Paul advised his shipmates—you will arrive safe and sound on the shore.

I am your God—the ultimate port in a storm. Look to me to surround you in my peace and shelter you in the harbor of my presence.

R e a d
A c t s 2 7 : 2 7 – 4 4 .

Safe in your arms, most capable God, is where I want to be.

We found believers and were invited to stay with them for seven days.

—**Acts 28:14** (HCSB)

FRIENDS IN OUT-OF-THE-WAY PLACES

I am *Jehovah-jireh,* the God who provides. I provide for you in more ways than you can count. Look at the friendships I have given you. When you have a need, I often move on someone around you to bless you. That's what I did for my beloved son Paul. I moved on the hearts of the people of Malta and the Christians of Puteoli to take care of him.

Child, I delight to provide for you in unexpected ways through my people. This is why you never have to worry about where I might send you. Just when you fear that you will be alone, I can bring you friends in out-of-the-way places. You are never beyond my ability to provide.

Read
Acts 28:1–16.

Precious God who supplies all, teach me to welcome the kindnesses of others.

NOVEMBER 19

*For the next two years, Paul
lived in Rome at his own
expense. He welcomed all who
visited him.*

—Acts 28:30 (NLT)

HOLY HOSPITALITY

P recious one, I love it when you are able to open your
home to simply share with others. I know you don't
always feel that your home is perfect enough, or your
cooking skills proficient enough, or your time plentiful
enough. But you, my child, are enough.

Hospitality is not about your house or your food—it's
about providing a place of love and enjoyment for others.
As you welcome guests into your less-than-perfect home
to enjoy a simple meal, you are following in a long
tradition. My children have always gladly welcomed
others. Over that meal, conversation occurs—about life,
about family, about the world, about me—and you have
opportunities to encourage or be encouraged, and perhaps
to introduce your friends to me.

And *my* hospitality is the best of all!

**Read
Acts 28:17–31.**

*Lord, I am willing
to extend the gift of
hospitality to all you
send my way.*

NOVEMBER 20

God demonstrates his own love for us in this: While we were still sinners, Christ died for us.
—**Romans 5:8** (NIV)

A DEMONSTRATION OF LOVE

My beautiful child, I treasure you and regard you as one would regard a rare and precious gem. My love for you is not determined by your actions, your skills, or what you can do for me. No, it is based on the fact that you are mine.

To demonstrate my love, I offered my Son's life to save yours—even when you didn't know you needed me. Even while sin had you in its clutches. Even before you were born. I knew you even then, and I sent my Son to die for you.

Oh child, I rejoice in our relationship, and I have such blessings to pour out on you! Look heavenward and open wide your arms, because showers of goodness are about to fall.

Read Romans 5:1–11.

Oh most holy God, fill me with your goodness.

You received the Spirit of son-ship. And by him we cry, "Abba, Father." —**Romans 8:15** (NIV)

BECAUSE I LOVE YOU

Because I have chosen you, I welcome you into my family as my child. I care for you and provide for as a good father would. I offer you a robe of righteousness bought through my Son's blood. I offer you a ring of status as my heir. And I offer you the mantle of my love, because perfect love drives away fear.

You are no longer a slave without status, bound to the dictates of the world. As my adopted child, you are under my protection and given my provision. Because you belong to me, I offer you the freedom and joy the world cannot offer. Best of all, I offer you the right to call me "Abba"—Daddy.

Because I love you.

**Read
Romans 8:1–17.**

Oh, Abba! Thank you for adopting me into your family.

NOVEMBER 22

*I am convinced that nothing
can ever separate us from God's
love.* —**Romans 8:38** (NLT)

LOVE ON DISPLAY

Nothing can keep my love from you, dear child. I am love. My nature is compassion, mercy, and grace. There is nothing you can do that will make me love you less, and nothing you can do to make me love you more.

If you ever question my love, look to the cross of Jesus. The boldest and grandest display of love made visible was in his sacrifice for your sins.

Look at the cross and see my love. Today and every day, remember that you are loved. Nothing will ever separate us—not life or death, not the spiritual powers of angels or demons, not your fears about today or your worries about tomorrow. Not even hell itself.

Nothing, absolutely nothing, can keep my love from you.

**Read
Romans 8:18–39.**

*Lord, help me
experience your
love today.*

NOVEMBER 23

Rejoice with those who rejoice;
mourn with those who mourn.
—**Romans 12:15** (NIV)

WALKING WITH OTHERS

People need you, special one. They need you to be there for them in the good times and the bad. As I walk with you on your journey and send people to be with you on the way, so I sometimes will guide you to walk the path with someone else.

At times it will be a path of rejoicing, and you will join in celebrating great joy in their lives. There's nothing quite like sharing a celebration with good friends. At other times the path will be dark and you will mourn with those who mourn. Great words of comfort won't be needed, but your presence will be.

Throughout the days of your lives, I give you one another. Just as some have walked the path with you, so walk the path with others. You have much to give.

Read
Romans 12.

Lord, help me to walk
the path with others,
caring for them.

*These three things continue
forever: faith, hope, and love.
And the greatest of these is love.*
—1 Corinthians 13:13 (NCV)

THE GREATEST OF THESE

My love for you does not end or grow weary. I chose to love you, chose to send my Son to die for you; I chose to have you as my precious child—willing love set into action.

As you show love toward others, think of the love I have for you. Love that is patient with foibles and failures. Love that shows kindness in a hard and sometimes rude world. Love that is not jealous or boastful or proud, but longs only for the very best. Love that is not rude but gracious, not selfish but selfless. Love that refuses to keep track of wrongs and always believes the best. Love that trusts, hopes, and perseveres.

Such love will never fail.

Read
1 Corinthians 13.

*Open my heart, Lord
God, to love others as
you have loved me.*

*Christ has indeed been raised
from the dead, the firstfruits of
those who have fallen asleep.*
—**1 Corinthians 15:20** (NIV)

THE TRIUMPH OF THE RESURRECTION

Death was not what I desired for my creation, but it
came as a result of disobedience in the garden. Yet
even then, I had a plan to snatch the victory from death.

Though it is a veil through which you must pass,
beloved, you will return to life. The resurrection of my
Son is your guarantee. He took your place on the cross
and rose victoriously from the dead. With one loving act
he broke the chains of sin and abolished death's hold.

Because my Son was raised, you can trust that you
too will be raised. He was the first of many, the first of all
my children who will be raised to eternal life with me.

Do not fear, my child. Eternity awaits you just on the
other side.

**Read
1 Corinthians
15:1 – 20.**

*Lord, please show me
someone to whom I can
talk about the triumph
of Jesus' resurrection.*

NOVEMBER 26

Thanks be to God, who gives us the victory through our Lord Jesus Christ.

—1 Corinthians 15:57 (NASB)

VICTORY!

Beloved, I gained the victory over sin and death. Sometimes it may not appear that way because of the evil and sadness in the world, but I have the final word. Sin and all its allure does not. Death and its seeming finality does not.

I love you so much that I sent my Son to bear the weight of your sin on the cross and to die in your place. Because of him your sin has been forgiven and death has been conquered. Now his triumph is yours.

Remember, I am the resurrection; I am the life. I reign supremely. The grave has no hold on me, for I have overcome it. So you need not fear death.

Read the final chapter of the story: *we win!* Walk with me and you will be safe, both now and for all eternity. You are a conqueror. So live victoriously.

Read
1 Corinthians
15:35–58.

Lord, Jesus' victory gives me hope and strength. I am grateful for the power to conquer.

*The things which are seen
are temporary, but the things
which are not seen are eternal.*
—**2 Corinthians 4:18** (NKJV)

SEEING INTO ETERNITY

Sometimes your pain can be so all-encompassing that it eclipses the light of my presence. But look beyond the pain, my child. Look for me. You are not alone, nor have you been forgotten.

I understand the suffering and sting of this world. I lost my beloved Son to the cruel machinery of a world gone mad. But I also overcame the darkness with life. Through my Spirit and the eyes of faith, you can look beyond your troubles—beyond the visible—and find me. I am still here. And, while you may not see me, I see you.

Everything that happens in this world is only for a moment in comparison to eternity. In heaven, my child, I will wipe away every tear you have ever shed. You will never experience pain again.

What you see is temporary. What you have with me is eternal.

**Read
2 Corinthians 4.** | *I will look to you today,
Lord, and focus on
what is to come, not
on what is.*

NOVEMBER 28

Let the Holy Spirit guide your lives. Then you won't be doing what your sinful nature craves.
—Galatians 5:16 (NLT)

I CAN GUIDE YOU

I know you sometimes struggle, feeling divided in mind and heart. One part of you wants to believe that ambition and worldly pleasure are the paths to happiness. But the other part knows that true joy is found only in following me.

Dear child, I am not forcing you to do things my way. I am holding out my hand to help you walk in the way that leads to life. With your hand in mine, you will have the strength to turn away from the distractions and temptations of the world.

I desire to lead you to a life of peace and joy. I want to give you patience and goodness, and enable you to be kind and faithful. I long to lead you in love.

Hold my hand and walk with me.

Read
Galatians 5:13–26.

Father, here is my hand. I trust you to lead me on the best path.

NOVEMBER 29

I pray that the eyes of your heart may be enlightened so you may know what is the hope of His calling.

—**Ephesians 1:18** (HCSB)

YOUR ETERNAL HOPE

Dear child, you may not realize it yet, but you are rich. I have prepared a treasure for you. In this treasure chest I have placed every possible spiritual blessing.

I planned this extravagant inheritance long before you were born. Even before I made the world, I chose you to be part of my family and to enjoy the family wealth. I took great pleasure in planning all this. I want you to experience the abundance of my kingdom.

I have given you my Spirit so that you may begin to understand the riches that are yours. Just ask. He will shine my light in your heart so that you can see more clearly the lavish treasure that is already yours.

Read Ephesians 1.

Giver of vision, open my eyes to see your extravagant gifts of love.

By grace you have been saved through faith. And this is not your own doing; it is the gift of God. —**Ephesians 2:8** (ESV)

CHERISH THE GIFT

E ven before you knew me or understood my ways, I prepared something special for you—the gift of faith. You didn't realize that you needed this gift, but I did. I knew you needed to trust in my Son, Jesus.

Sometimes it is difficult to receive a present; you'd rather work for it or earn it. But faith is not something you can earn. I purchased the gift of faith for you with the blood of my own Son.

Because I love you, it has been my joy to plan this present for you. Because I cherish you, I delighted in preparing it. Because I treasure you, I wanted to give you what is precious and valuable. So I took this gift of faith, wrapped it in my mercy and grace, and tied the package with my love.

Cherish the gift.

Read Ephesians 2.

Father, thank you for the precious gift of faith. Jesus, thank you for paying the price.

DECEMBER

DECEMBER 1

Christ gave those gifts to prepare
God's holy people for the work
of serving, to make the body of
Christ stronger. —**Ephesians**
4:12 (NCV)

A GIFT FOR YOU

People love to give gifts when babies are born, and in the same way, I love to give gifts when sons or daughters are born anew into my family. These gifts are special abilities for serving my kingdom. Gifts that reach out to those who don't yet know me, and that help my children grow closer to me.

I give different abilities because I love to watch my children blend their gifts together in my name. All are important. One gifted person needs other gifted people in order to get the job done.

When you use your gift, you honor me. If you're not sure what your gift is, talk to me and to others who know and love you. I'll show you, my child. After all, I have special plans for you!

Read
Ephesians 4:1–16.

Lord, show me my gift,
then show me how to
use it for you.

Put on the full armor of God, so that when the day of evil comes, you may be able to stand your ground. —**Ephesians 6:13** (NIV)

PREPARED FOR THE BATTLE

My child, you are in a battle. This is no ordinary battle, for you cannot see your adversary. The conflict is no less real, however—the forces of evil are constantly waging war in the spiritual realm.

I have provided you with the best equipment available to fight this spiritual battle. The belt of truth, to defend you from the enemy's lies. Layers of righteousness and integrity, to protect your heart. The shoes of my peace, readying you to share. The shield of faith, for when Satan sends fiery arrows your way. The helmet of salvation, to secure your mind from doubting who you are in me. The sword of my Word, to fight off Satan's attacks and conquer his lies.

Dress daily in my armor, precious one. It will protect you.

Read
Ephesians
6:10–20.

Lord, I thank you for giving me the armor necessary to fight all battles.

DECEMBER 3

*In your lives you must think
and act like Christ Jesus.*
—**Philippians 2:5** (NCV)

THE PATH OF HONOR

In this world the desire for more privileges and greater admiration is tempting. But dear one, this is not my way. In my kingdom, the road to honor is the path of humility.

As you walk this path, let others go before you. In fact, help others to get ahead. Don't demand the best position; be willing to go last. The path of humility may mean doing work no one else wants, jobs that earn no reward, duties that seem beneath you. But as you walk on my road, leaving behind your desire for attention, I will applaud you. Let go of your pride and I will cheer you on.

After all, that is how my Son lived. When you humble yourself before me, I promise to lift you up.

Read
Philippians
2:1–18.

*Lord, lead me on
your humble path to
heavenly honor.*

DECEMBER 4

Dear brothers and sisters,
pattern your lives after mine,
and learn from those who follow
our example. —**Philippians**
3:17 (NLT)

YOUR MODEL LIFE

Whether you realize it or not, others are observing your walk with me. You do not have to be perfect in order to be a good example; just walk with me. That will be enough to make you stand out from your world. I planned it that way.

My children are different. They have my Spirit within them; they have eternity in their hearts; they have hope and a future. So, my child, walk with me and live as an example. When you stumble, admit the mistake and move on. (That, too, is an example to others.) Let them see what a difference knowing me makes in handling both the joys and the difficulties of life.

As we walk together, more people will be drawn to you. Our friendship will cause others to want to know more about us—and then you can tell them our story.

Read
Philippians 3.

Intimate Friend, I
draw close to you. May
my life be a model for
others.

DECEMBER 5

See to it that no one takes you captive through hollow and deceptive philosophy.

—**Colossians 2:8** (NIV)

COME TO MY STOREHOUSE

My child, the world extols self-help methods and hidden teachings as the means to gaining a "higher" knowledge. But any avenue to understanding apart from me is a trapdoor leading to an empty room.

I invite you to check all other ideas and philosophies against my Word. I am the source of true knowledge, ready and waiting to impart my insight to you. By trusting me, you are not surrendering your ability to think and reason. Instead, I enhance your understanding, for there is no end to my storehouse of knowledge.

Meet me in my Word. Bring your toughest questions. Come, let's reason together.

Read
Colossians 2:1–15.

All-wise Father, help me to ignore all empty knowledge. I look to you for wisdom.

DECEMBER 6

Set your hearts on things above,
where Christ is seated at the
right hand of God.

—**Colossians 3:1** (NIV)

LOOK UP

I have given you a brand-new life. Your spiritual rebirth makes you a citizen of my kingdom and puts you under my loving protection. Though your body is on earth, your real life is with me in heaven.

Keep your eyes fixed on me, and I will help you cling to things of everlasting value. As you focus on your invisible life, your visible life will also change. You will begin to shed unrighteous anger, unforgiveness, and pride. Your life will shine with increasing kindness, humility, and love. Others will seek the light you reflect.

I am here, eager to teach you about this authentic life. Look up, my love.

Read
Colossians 3:1–17.

Lord, thank you for the
gift of a resurrected
life. Center my thoughts
on you.

The word of the Lord is ringing out from you to people everywhere. —**1 Thessalonians 1:8** (NLT)

THE NEWS OF YOUR FAITH

Child of mine, I have chosen you to be my bell—tolling the good news of my Son. You may not see yourself as an example of strong faith, but remember: I do not require perfect faith or a litany of well-rehearsed answers. You can simply show others how faith in me has changed your life. You can explain how what you worshiped before is no longer important to you, now that you know *me*—the only living God.

Today, let others see how you depend on me. I long to share my strength with them too.

Let your speech and life proclaim my love. The news of your faith will touch the lives of others, ringing the good news from your life to everyone around you!

Read
1 Thessalonians
1:2–10.

Father, may my words and actions speak of your love.

We shall always be with the Lord.

—**1 Thessalonians 4:17** (NKJV)

FOREVER

I know the deep sorrows in life, precious one. Death and loss. Grief and tragedy. Heartache and mourning. These are part of life on earth.

I know you miss those dear to you who have passed away. And I know you are concerned about the end of your own life. Yet always, there is hope. I crushed the power of death and freed all who trust in me from its effect. Death cannot hold down anyone who believes in the power of my resurrection.

Soon we will all be together in heaven. Those who have gone before you will be there too. So don't grieve as if you will never see them again. Your sorrow will have an end. Your loved ones will be with me. You will be with me.

Forever.

Read
1 Thessalonians 4.

Risen Lord, thank you for defeating death. I look forward to forever.

*We can't help but thank God
for you, because your faith is
flourishing and your love for
one another is growing.*

—2 Thessalonians 1:3 (NLT)

FLOURISHING FAITH

Dear child, I have a gardener's eye in regard to your
faith. Use tough times to nourish your trust in
me. Let the winds of hardship deepen your roots in my
faithfulness. Allow driving rain to water your confidence
in me.

I will strengthen your roots and help you to stretch
out in love to your family, friends, and neighbors.
Reaching out will cultivate your reliance on me and
increase your love, not just for those who share your
affection but for those who are difficult to love, who are
distant or demanding.

I take joy in your flourishing faith and abounding
affection. Through you, I am reaping a harvest for
eternity.

Read
2 Thessalonians 1.

*Help me to develop
strong roots of trust
and flourishing faith.*

DECEMBER 10

As for the rest of you, dear brothers and sisters, never get tired of doing good. —**2 Thessalonians 3:13** (NLT)

I SEE, I KNOW

Don't despair when you struggle to do the right thing and wonder if your efforts are making a difference. I notice every caring act. I see the blessing that you are, and I am with you, encouraging you to continue being a blessing.

When you show goodness toward others, you help to change the world for the better. Kindness in my name lets others know that I care. A gentle touch may help someone get through the day. Even a simple smile can encourage a heart drowning in sorrow.

Keep reaching out to others. Continue to spread my love. Maintain a spirit of kindness and compassion. I will give you strength to carry on.

Never tire of doing good. I never tire of showing my goodness to you.

Read
2 Thessalonians
3:6–18.

I'm tired, Lord. Grant me the strength to persevere with deeds of love.

*Physical training is good, but
training for godliness is much
better, promising benefits in
this life and in the life to come.*
—1 Timothy 4:8 (NLT)

SPIRITUALLY FIT

Dear one, physical workouts are necessary to
maintain health in this life. But training in
godliness will bless you in this life and the next. Trust me
to work my character in you and train your mind until my
attitudes become yours. Let my Spirit coach you in faith
and goodness.

I long to see you spiritually fit. You can exercise your
spirit by meditating on my Word and spending time with
fellow believers. I invite you to come to me for regular
consultations on your spiritual health.

Committing to this training will reap eternal rewards.
I am with you every step of the way because I love you.

Read
1 Timothy 4.

*Heavenly Coach, train
me to be more like you.
Exercise my spirit in
godliness.*

Flee from all this, and pursue
righteousness, godliness, faith,
love, endurance and gentleness.
Fight the good fight of faith.
—**1 Timothy 6:11–12** (NIV)

PURSUE ME

The world is filled with so many temptations: the love of money, the quest for power, the craving for importance. All of these can lead you away from true faith and on a path toward evil.

You are my beloved lamb—a sheep from my fold. Run from the snares of the world and into the safety of my pasture. I will be with you as you chase after a stronger faith, aim for a deeper love, exercise perseverance, and search out gentleness. This kind of living will lead you to my great riches: satisfaction, fulfillment, contentment, peace. Riches that I, the Good Shepherd, lovingly provide for my sheep.

Pursue me, beloved.

Read
1 Timothy 6:6–19.

Lord, I run to you now
on the path of joy.

DECEMBER 13

God gave us a spirit not of fear but of power and love and self-control. —**2 Timothy 1:7** (ESV)

NO MORE FEAR

Child, when the sun rises, the darkness flees. No darkness can withstand the power of the light. Fear is like that fleeing night. It is but a shadow, a smoke-screen that temporarily hides the light.

Through the blood of my Son, I have made you a conqueror with a message of truth. Like Timothy, you are charged with teaching the truth to others in the ways to which I have called you.

When fear rises up, you have the power to conquer it through the name of my Son. You have my Spirit within you, fueling you with love and equipping you as needs arise.

Come to me with your fear, and I will give you the power to see beyond it and to move beyond it—dispelling the darkness with my light.

Read
2 Timothy 1:1–14.

Lord, help me to be bold in witnessing to the truth of your love.

DECEMBER 14

All Scripture is God-breathed and is useful for teaching, rebuking, correcting and training in righteousness. —**2 Timothy 3:16** (NIV)

BREATH OF LIFE

My breath gave life to Adam when I formed him from the earth. It gave life to you the day you were born, and gave you new life through my Spirit when you became my child.

That life-giving breath is also found in my Word. I breathed it into my servants who wrote my words, the words I wanted people to read. Scripture bears my breath—my power. My Word gives life, brings peace, shows the way, offers guidance and encouragement and, above all, tells you more about me.

My child, I entrust my Book to you. Through it you can hear me communicate to you. I have much to share with you. Let's read together.

Read
2 Timothy 3.

Breathe on me, breath of God. Let me hear your words in your Word.

DECEMBER 15

He saved us, not because of righteous things we had done, but because of his mercy.

—**Titus 3:8** (NIV)

BECAUSE OF MY MERCY

I am characterized by mercy. Some people don't understand that. They see me as unyielding or unloving or distant. They do not know me as you know me, child. I am a compassionate God, always desiring to forgive, always drawing people to myself, always offering second chances—and more. Why? Because I love. Because I long to save.

Plenty of people seek to be "good enough" for me, but the truth is, no one could ever be that good. So in my mercy I made a way through my sinless, holy Son. I draw people to myself, give them salvation, and help them to become more like my Son every day as they walk with me.

I saved you, not because you were good enough, but because of my mercy. It's who I am.

Read
Titus 3:1–11.

Merciful God, thank you for your mercy that saved me.

DECEMBER 16

Let us not give up meeting to-gether, as some are in the habit of doing, but let us encourage one another. —**Hebrews 10:25** (NIV)

STANDING AS ONE

Dearest one, while the enemy of your soul seeks to bring division, I provide unity. I have built a community of believers called the church and given them my power. Where two or more are gathered, I am in their midst. I provide the love that draws this family together and the common purpose that compels them to work to build my kingdom.

It does my heart good when my children meet to encourage one another. Together you can accomplish more than you can on your own. You keep each other accountable and support each other through the network of gifts offered by my Spirit.

I know sometimes difficulties arise, but don't give up on one another. When you stand as one, I stand with you.

Read Hebrews 10:19–39.

Lord God, I will stand with my brothers and sisters. Together, we will prevail.

Anyone who comes to him must believe that he exists and that he rewards those who earnestly seek him. —**Hebrews 11:6** (NIV)

BEYOND SIGHT

Faith is a bend in the road that takes you beyond sight. It is a step along the precipice of fear, yet a step protected by the knowledge that I am there with you.

I know you seek answers, beloved. You live in a world powered by the notion that seeing is believing. But I offer you more. I offer a patience that makes your faith steady and unflappable. And I offer to reveal my glory in you, growing brighter, so that everyone around you gets a glimpse of me.

How I long for you to see your obstacles, heartbreaks, and struggles for what they are: opportunities to seek me on your knees and experience my grace. Whatever comes, earnestly look to me, asking for help to believe. Many saints throughout history can testify: I will take care of the rest.

Read
Hebrews 11:1–13.

Thank you, Abba Father, that when I earnestly seek you, you make faith possible.

Discipline . . . yields the peaceful
fruit of righteousness to those
who have been trained by it.
—**Hebrews 12:11** (ESV)

GOOD ON YOU

Dearest, if I did not love you, I would not discipline
you. Would any father who truly loved his child
allow that child to act in rude or harmful ways?

As your loving Father, I watch over you as you
mature in your faith and walk with me. I want you to
grow strong in me and to live in a manner worthy of your
calling. I want to guide you on the right path, showing you
the ways that honor me and keep you safe. Sometimes I
need to make things a little difficult for you, to help you
understand. But don't be discouraged: each instance of
my correction offers you a chance to take hold of stronger
faith, a straight path, and the healing and peace that come
with righteousness.

You see, I love you so much that I will allow short-
term pain to bring you long-term peace.

Read
Hebrews 12:1–13.

Heavenly Father, thank
you for a love that
wounds, then heals.

DECEMBER 19

If any of you need wisdom, you should ask God, and it will be given to you. —**James 1:5** (CEV)

SIMPLY ASK

You need wisdom, dear one, to manage life's challenges. I am your source. Look to me.

Sometimes the way isn't clear, the answers seem vague, the questions seem indecipherable. I take great pleasure in giving you everything you need to live honorably, rightly, peacefully in your world, beginning with wisdom. Look to me.

You need wisdom. Wisdom helps to clarify. It separates right from wrong, good from bad. It discerns the best path out of many. So look to me.

When you need wisdom, ask. I will give it to you without holding back.

Read
James 1.

Father, I need wisdom from you today.

DECEMBER 20

*It is good when you obey the royal law as found in the Scriptures: "Love your neighbor as yourself." —***James 2:8** (NLT)

HEARTBEAT OF LOVE

Just as my heart beats for the brokenhearted and my hands uphold the least among you, I long for you to pour yourself out for the poor, the marginalized, the oppressed. When you generously care for them, you fulfill my law. When you honor them, you honor my name. When you show them mercy, my heart sings and heaven rejoices.

Embrace the upside-down virtues of my kingdom and lift up those who have little. Though they have little, they are loved much. Love them as you love yourself. In extending unexpected kindness and mercy to those who cannot help themselves, you will find that my mercy overflows to you, overwhelming you with goodness and grace.

Read James 2:1–13.

Lord, your mercy overwhelms me—help me to share it lavishly with those who have little.

DECEMBER 21

No one can tame the tongue; it is a restless evil and full of deadly poison. —**James 3:8** (NASB)

TO TAME A TONGUE

You know from experience that words can help and words can hurt. I have witnessed others hurting your heart through their speech. I know the times when words have wounded you. I know when you have said words you wanted to take back. It is difficult to tame a tongue—to make it a tool for blessing. But how my heart longs for you to deliver words fitly spoken, seasoned with grace, imbued with goodness and power!

What is the secret to taming an unruly tongue? *I AM.* When you love me, and meditate on my words, and follow after me, your thoughts become like my thoughts. Changed words follow changed thinking. My Spirit inside of you bubbles up, overflows, and spills out through lips that speak words of life and healing.

Read
James 3:1–12.

Father, tame my tongue so it brings life and healing.

DECEMBER 22

*You are a chosen people, a royal
priesthood, a holy nation, a
people belonging to God.*

—1 Peter 2:9 (NIV)

YOU ARE MINE

Let me remind you of who you are and help you
embrace your identity as my child. Everything
changed between us when you asked my Son to be your
Savior and Lord. I sought you out, wanting to adopt you
into my family, and you responded to my invitation. In
that moment you became not only my child but a priest—
someone with the privilege of calling on me directly at any
time. You were appointed to do my work and show the
world what it means to be chosen.

You are royalty, a child of the King. You are holy,
for my Son died to take away your sin. And you, precious
one, are mine.

Read
1 Peter 2:1–10.

*Father, help my life
to praise you and my
heart to remember
whose I am.*

*It is better to suffer for doing
good, if that is what God wants,
than to suffer for doing wrong!*
—**1 Peter 3:17** (NLT)

THE TRIUMPH OF SUFFERING

Blessed are those, my dear child, who are persecuted
for following my Son. It is easy to follow me when
no one opposes you, when linking with me appears to be
both logical and popular. But when you are mistreated for
honoring my name, discouragement can easily give way to
anger. Ask me for help to resist it! There is no one—and
nothing—to fear. You can rely on me.

I see all, knowing even your unuttered prayers, and
I promise that any goodness done in my name will not
be wasted. I have provided all that you need to respond
with gentleness, faithfulness, and confidence: my ultimate
victory is sure.

Embrace the triumph of suffering for me, as my son
Peter did. Your heavenly crown will shine all the brighter
for it.

Read
1 Peter 3:8–22.

*King of my heart, let
any suffering I face
bring honor to you.*

DECEMBER 24

*God has given us everything
we need for living a godly life.*
—**2 Peter 1:3** (NLT)

GIFTED

Beloved, I have riches for you that are simply for
the taking. Just as you wouldn't leave a present
unwrapped, I would not want you to leave my promises
untouched.

As Peter neared his life's end, he testified that my
power was the source of all spiritual victory and abundant
life. You can know this truth for yourself. Just stick
close to me. Your godliness will increase as you put my
precious promises into practice. Through the power of my
Spirit I will add goodness to your faith and self-control
to the knowledge I impart, along with perseverance and
kindness.

As you move nearer to the day when you will see
my face, keep on shining for me. The greatest gift of all
awaits.

Read
2 Peter 1:3–21.

*Thank you for the
precious gift of
salvation, O Lord.
Help me to treasure
and share it.*

If we confess our sins to God, he can always be trusted to forgive us and take our sins away.
—1 John 1:9 (CEV)

A FRESH START

Come and drink deep in the well of belief. Know that even when you do wrong, I am still here for you. Come to me. Talk to me. Tell me what is on your heart. I already know anyway, so we might as well get things out in the open where we can deal with them.

You see, when you confess your sins, it shows me that you understand what was wrong. When your heart is repentant, I clear the slate and send your sin as far as the east is from the west—forgiven and forgotten.

All your sins have already been covered at the cross, washed by the blood of my beloved Son. So come to me, my child. I can heal and forgive and make you clean.

Receive my grace. Each confession ushers in a fresh start.

Read
1 John 1.

Father, I'm overwhelmed by your mercy and thankful for your ever-forgiving heart.

DECEMBER 26

Little children, let us not love in word or talk but in deed and in truth. —1 John 3:18 (ESV)

IN DEED AND IN TRUTH

You are my child by faith, and your faith shows itself in how you live. Your deep faith in me causes you to *act*: to serve a brother or sister in need, to offer a second chance to someone who has offended you, to go where I send you. And because of my willing sacrifice for you, faith even motivates you to be willing to lay down your life for a friend.

I can see in your heart that your love is more than words. It shows up in your life, your actions, your reactions, your attitudes. Your desire to serve me honors me. As you love in deed and in truth, you show a watching world my kind of love—love that lasts.

Read
1 John 2:28 – 3:23.

Abba, your love for me is amazing; help me to show my love for you today by my actions.

DECEMBER 27

Loving God means keeping his commandments, and his commandments are not burdensome.
—1 John 5:3 (NLT)

LOVE AND OBEY

In addition to the spiritual armor I have crafted for you, I have given you a garment that fits all seasons and under any conditions. That garment is my love. A protective covering crafted especially for you, it offers comfort in every circumstance, and its flexibility brings freedom, ease of movement, and eternal peace to all who wear it. So when I ask you to respond to my love by obeying me and keeping my commandments, I am not requesting anything that is ill-fitting, impossible, or heavy. As the true Lover of your soul, I want only what is best for you—and following my commandments really *is* best, my child.

Love and obey. That's all I ask.

Read
1 John 5.

Lord, clothe me in obedience as I walk in your love.

DECEMBER 28

We ought to support [traveling teachers], that we may be fellow workers of the truth.

—3 John 8 (ESV)

MY HANDS

I am pleased when you encourage those servants of mine who travel far and wide to spread the truth of my Son to thirsty hearts. I have called them to give up much for the sake of my kingdom, a task they have gladly accepted. And I have called you to help them—to be a refuge, strength, and comfort along their way.

Be hospitable, child. Open your heart and your home. When you welcome them, you are welcoming me. When you offer a listening ear, you are *my* ear, giving my servants much-needed encouragement. When you meet their needs, you are *my* hands, helping ease my servants' load. When you bless them with a warm meal, a comfortable bed, and the joy of conversation, you are blessing me.

As you open yourself to serving my servants, you are building my kingdom as well.

Read 3 John.

Lord, show me how to bless your servants out of the abundance of what you have given me.

Look, he is coming with the clouds, and every eye will see him. . . . So shall it be! Amen.
—**Revelation 1:7** (NIV)

I AM COMING BACK!

Precious one, some truths about me are so powerful—so life-altering—that they inspire an "Amen!" or a "So be it, Lord." My son John knew that the greatest truth ever told about me is this: *I am coming back!*

Many wonder why the world is such a mess and how I can let it be that way if I really love people. They are asking for a perfect world—and one day that is exactly what I will bring. The world will not stay as it is; I am coming to make all things new. Everyone will see my return. You and all my children who have joined my family will rejoice, for it will be a time of joy like no one has ever seen.

Wait for it, child. The day is coming. That's a promise.

Read
Revelation 1.

I am watching expectantly for your return.

He will wipe away every tear from their eyes. —**Revelation 21:4** (ESV)

I WILL WIPE AWAY YOUR TEARS

B eloved, one day I will gently touch your face and wipe away your tears. Tears you've shed in sorrow over sin. Tears over the pain in your heart from regret. Tears for the loss of loved ones to sickness and death. Tears from the hurt that people inflicted upon you. Tears of frustration and anger.

I know about tears; my Son wept at the grave of his beloved friend Lazarus. One day tears will be no more. There will be no more reason to cry, for I will remove all of that regret and loss and hurt and frustration and anger. Gone.

I will replace your sorrows with myself, my love, my presence.

I will make all things new.

Read
Revelation 21.

Father, I long for your presence when you will wipe away all my tears.

DECEMBER 31

Listen! I am coming soon! I will bring my reward with me, and I will repay each one of you for what you have done.

—Revelation 22:12 (NCV)

SOON!

My Son will return! As promised, he is coming for you and the rest of my family.

As much as we all long for this joyous reunion, you do not have to stand there watching the sky as Jesus' disciples did on the day he returned to heaven. Instead, I have a job for you. Keep communicating with me, and keep taking in my love. As you receive this love, lavish it on others, especially the least among you. Keep imitating my Son and being led by my Spirit. These are the actions that will be rewarded in eternity.

Jesus is coming for you, dear one. This is a promise your heart can rest in fully as you watch, listen, and serve.

The rooms are ready, the gate is open. I can't wait to wrap you in my arms.

Read
Revelation
22:7–21.

Heavenly Father, I can't wait to be in your arms!